ADIRONDA~ 〜〜 E
〜 ✧ **W9-CIM-530**
〜 ~~〜

Philosophical and Ethical Problems in Mental Handicap

Also by Peter Byrne

COMPANION ENCYCLOPEDIA OF THEOLOGY (*co-editor with J. L. Houlden*)
ETHICS AND LAW IN HEALTH CARE AND RESEARCH (*editor*)
HEALTH, RIGHTS AND RESOURCES (*editor*)
MEDICINE AND CONTEMPORARY SOCIETY (*editor*)
MEDICINE, MEDICAL ETHICS AND THE VALUE OF LIFE (*editor*)
THE MORAL INTERPRETATION OF RELIGION
NATURAL RELIGION AND THE NATURE OF RELIGION
* THE PHILOSOPHICAL AND THEOLOGICAL FOUNDATIONS OF ETHICS
* PROLEGOMENA TO RELIGIOUS PLURALISM
* RELIGION DEFINED AND EXPLAINED (*with Peter B. Clarke*)
RIGHTS AND WRONGS IN MEDICINE (*editor*)

* *From the same publishers*

Philosophical and Ethical Problems in Mental Handicap

Peter Byrne
Professor of Ethics and the Philosophy of Religion
King's College London

Published by PALGRAVE
Houndmills, Basingstoke, Hampshire RG21 6XS and
175 Fifth Avenue, New York, N.Y. 10010
Companies and representatives throughout the world

PALGRAVE is the new global academic imprint of
St. Martin's Press LLC Scholarly and Reference Division and
Palgrave Publishers Ltd (formerly Macmillan Press Ltd).

Outside North America
ISBN 0–333–80116–4

In North America
ISBN 0–312–23460–0

This book is printed on paper suitable for recycling and made from fully managed and sustained forest sources.

A catalogue record for this book is available from the British Library.

Library of Congress Catalog Card Number: 00–027830

10   9   8   7   6   5   4   3   2
09   08   07   06   05   04   03   02   01

Printed and bound in Great Britain by
Antony Rowe Ltd, Eastbourne

Contents

Preface

> Equality is a vital need of the human soul. It consists in a cognition, at once public, general, effective and genuinely expressed in institutions and customs, that the same amount of respect and consideration is due to every being because this respect is due to the human being as such and it is not a matter of degree. It follows that the inevitable differences among men ought never to imply any difference in the degree of respect.[1]

It is fashionable nowadays for authors in the humanities to state the standpoint from which they are writing before presenting their arguments and conclusions on a topic. In the interests of maintaining my reputation for being modish, I wish to explain the sources of my interest in the philosophical and ethical dimensions of mental handicap.

One major source was a confrontation early in my academic career with the burgeoning subject of 'philosophical medical ethics' or 'bioethics'. That discipline has a prime interest in the question of the value of human life and the moral status of human beings. This interest manifests itself in discussions of many aspects of medical practice. For example, we find the question of the value of human life to the fore in debates about the ethics of medical and scientific research – in particular when the differences in the treatment of human beings and animals as subjects of medical research are addressed.

The question is posed as to why we (that is, the majority of people in Western societies) feel that animals can be treated in ways that cannot be contemplated for human subjects. The standard answer to that query posits a difference between the moral status of animals and humans based on the latter's characteristic possession of qualities such as self-consciousness, reason and autonomy. This grounding for a distinctive research ethics for human beings is linked to customary distinctions between an ethics to govern the killing of animals and one for homicide. However, the grounding of differential status in the possession of higher functions of intelligence and agency naturally raises the question of the moral status of human beings who appear to lack those higher functions to some degree or other. It is in this way that I was introduced many years ago to the question of why we should give the mentally handicapped, or more precisely *all* the mentally handicapped, the unique moral status afforded to human beings. This source of philosophical enquiry into the nature of mental handicap will be explored in greater detail in Chapter 1.

A second stimulus to my interest in these topics arose through the chance reading of a book by David Pailin: *A Gentle Touch*. This book made me consider two thoughts which I had not previously entertained. One thought was that the difficulties in answering the philosophical question as to the moral status of the mentally handicapped might evaporate if we bring in theology. Perhaps the worth of all human beings does not rest on their intrinsic qualities, but rather on the fact that they are the objects of divine love. A second thought Pailin made me consider is that there may in reality be no useful distinction served by the contrast between the able and the disabled, the normal and the handicapped. The first idea derived from Pailin made the resolution of the philosophical problem of the moral status of the mentally handicapped more pressing for me, since I am not a religious believer. The second made me think about the very possibility of giving a sense to the notion of 'the mentally handicapped'.

The stimuli to my thinking mentioned so far raised in my mind the underlying issue of this study, namely: what is the relation between the notions of the human and of the (mentally) handicapped? Our thinking on this question reveals an apparent tension. On the one hand, customary morality and the common law want to give the mentally handicapped the basics of what pertains to the human. They are not to be treated like animals. There is, for example, no special category of homicide in customary morality and common law relating to killing one who is mentally impaired. On the other hand, the very distinction we make between the normal and retarded human being – a distinction to which great social consequences may be attached – implies that they are not to be regarded as we regard normal human beings. A central thesis of this book is that the notion of the common humanity of all of us is the only sound basis for an ethics which embraces all we regard as handicapped and yet is also the means for recognising the appropriate differences between the many who are not mentally handicapped and the few who are.

The third stimulus for this study was the birth of my second son, Gareth. Gareth displayed significant delays in language acquisition in the latter half of his second year and was, after the presentation of further symptoms, diagnosed as autistic by his third birthday. He has since those early days given me graphic displays of the fact that we may all share a common humanity yet display the most fundamental differences in cognition, communication and behaviour. Gareth's existence explains why there are frequent references to autism in this book.

There is a danger in introducing so personal note into a survey of conceptual and ethical issues. It would be quite wrong to suppose that any of the arguments on matters relating to mental handicap which follow are the sounder or more persuasive because their author has a child with a disability. They must of course stand or fall on their merits. However, Gareth's existence does have a twofold role in the remainder of this story. In the first place, he may reassure the reader that the author has some experience of mental handicap, albeit that it is limited to one, special instance of that category. In the second place, Gareth explains a fundamental ethical commitment underlying the arguments which follow. It is the commitment so clearly and eloquently signalled in the quotation from Simone Weil at the head of this Preface. This book will endorse throughout the notion that those whom we classify as mentally handicapped are just as much persons as the rest of us. They are persons because they are human beings. To affirm their personhood will come down, in later chapters, to affirming that there is a range of obligations we owe to them, obligations which commit us to respecting their lives and working to make their flourishing possible. These are obligations owed to all human beings as such and falling on any human community as such. It is a fact about my experience that I cannot see matters in any way but this. This fact is down to Gareth.

It follows from the above fundamental commitment that this study will not endorse any of the many views fashionable in philosophical medical ethics or bioethics which affirm that not all human beings are persons (that is: that not all human beings are worthy of the moral respect just described). On the philosophers' account human beings who have not yet attained self-consciousness and autonomy, or who will never attain them, or who have lost them are not to count as persons. Chapter 3 of this study is devoted to rebutting the claim that not all human beings are persons. Since this chapter is crucial in the book's entire argument, it is worth setting out its plot now.

My rebuttal of the philosophers' dismissal of the ethical significance of humanity contains a range of arguments functioning at different levels. One level of argument is very simple. It consists in an appeal to what we would ordinarily say plus an attempt to refute the main reasons philosophers offer for rejecting what we ordinarily say. Appeal is made to our everyday sense that killing infants and the mentally handicapped is murder. It is noted that philosophers endeavour to set aside such ordinary reactions by two means. In the first place, they categorise them as 'intuitions' (where that implies that they must give way if plausible theoretical considerations so dictate). In the second place, they argue that to judge that all human beings are persons entails the adoption of 'speciesism'. Speciesism is the alleged intellectual and moral vice of regarding membership of the human race as decisive and necessary for moral worth. It is held to be morally on a par with racism. I contend against the first of these arguments that our ordinary moral judgements on something as fundamental as the wrongness of killing infants and the handicapped are not properly represented as intuitions. This reply allows that it may be possible to show that such judgements are confused or prejudiced but it aims to reset the balance between judgements about the rights and wrongs of actions, on the one hand, and philosophical theories of a general kind, on the other. Against the appeal to the vice of speciesism, the second section of Chapter 3 offers a diagnosis of the speciesism charge as a piece of philosophical confusion which is riddled with fallacy.

Thus far the argument in Chapter 3 is straightforward: a reminder of what we customarily think about the wrongness of killing any human being plus an attempt to rebut objections to that stance. The third section offers a positive reason for regarding all human beings as having moral worth. This argument is grounded upon the assertion that all human beings are possessed of a common species-nature. The inherent value of all human beings is a reflection of the value of the rational nature which they all possess. That nature is present in human beings from birth to death and so they are to be valued at all stages of their development. It is present in the mentally handicapped, though in them it is impaired.

The positive argument just outlined provides a philosophical basis for the assertion of the moral equality of all human beings provided by Simone Weil. The argument faces objections, and some of these are noted and discussed in Chapter 3. However, the further argument which closes the chapter is likely to seem more problematical still to many readers. In the closing sections of the chapter I develop a line of reasoning inherent in the writings of David Cockburn, Cora Diamond, Rai Gaita and Anne Maclean cited in the Bibliography at the close of this work. This line of reasoning constitutes a yet sharper objection to the way philosophers have argued about the rights and wrongs of killing human beings. The objection amounts to a rejection of the fundamental approach analytical philosophy has developed in its recent forays into practical ethics. The approach aims to provide a philosophical commentary on customary judgements about rights and wrongs. It does so by seeking to establish through philosophical theorising what things (more especially, lives) have value and what things (lives) do not. With that account of what is of value, the philosopher can re-enter the moral arena with a body of assured principles and interrogate customary moral opinions and categories accordingly.

Negatively, the closing sections of Chapter 3 (and the literature they draw on) contend that there is neither clarity nor certainty in such philosophical theories of the valuable. Such clarity and certainty as they have arises from their tacit dependence on moral judgements and categories available to us in ordinary moral language. They appear to offer a use of moral reason which transcends customary moral judgements and categories. In reality, however, the only valid use of moral reason is an immanent one. A reader of this book in draft complained that this way of summing up the matter is a retreat into 'wisespeak' but I hope that the distinction between transcendent and immanent uses of moral reason is clear in context.

Positively, the closing sections of the chapter aim to indicate how moral reactions to the handicapped such as compassion are revelatory of the value of the handicapped. As such, these reactions are more certain guides as to rights and wrongs than philosophical theories. This runs absolutely counter to the way in which our 'feelings' towards the afflicted are treated by philosophical theorists. I connect the revelatory character of compassion and the like to a sense of the afflicted as sharing a common life or lot with us. The revelation of value is bound up with a sense of shared relationship.

This way of describing the grounding of value is further linked to various attempts to fix the character of love (for example, the love parents of a mentally handicapped child may show to it in a lifetime of care) as revelatory of value. The effect of all this is to tie appropriate moral reflection in this area more closely still to the customary ways of feeling, judging and perceiving which philosophical ethics regards with so much scorn.

Murky stuff! Why dabble in it? I hope the murk is not too dense, but rather that in the context of the argument of the entire book and its subject matter of how we should treat the mentally handicapped it will be comprehensible to a degree. One of the major reasons why it is there (over and above the fact that the writings of Cockburn *et al.* on this score seem to me convincing) is that I find that the character of my experience with Gareth points me in this direction. That is, I cannot make sense of that experience unless I accept that love and its associated attitudes are revelatory of value and unless the fact of common membership of a human community tells morally in the way I suggest in Chapter 3. What the closing sections of the chapter above all testify to is a refusal on my part to credit that a philosophical theory of the valuable or of 'moral status' gives us any more moral insight, or any more certainty in discerning what we owe to a human being, than our perception of another as an afflicted, fellow human being. The theories of bioethics examined in Chapter 1 imply that the loving devotion of parents nurturing a handicapped infant or the dedication shown in teachers and therapists in endeavouring to give an autistic child the rudiments of speech is misguided (at least, misguided if it is thought to be demanded by its object). The latter half of Chapter 3 is meant to give some support, however feeble, to the sense I have that no philosophical theory has shown that. At no stage do I rule out someone showing that some of our fundamental ways of acting were prejudiced or otherwise morally corrupt. What I object to is the method adopted by many bioethicists in pursuit of that end.

My feeling that the 'murk' contained in Chapter 3 is preferable to the philosophical clarity of bioethics is down to Gareth. The developing argument of Chapter 3 is an attempt to fuse the experience of being the parent of a disabled child with the responsibilities of a philosopher to offer a discursive argument on matters of ethical and social import. As such an attempt at fusing the perspectives of philosopher and parent, it is a failure. But it is the best I can do at the moment. If the book is read by anyone who is provoked thereby to do a better job at such mediation, then it will have succeeded.

The reader who provided the comment on the murky character of the second half of Chapter 3 ('wisespeak') also suggested that the book is liable merely to preach to the converted. While those readers who find the philosophically grounded conclusions of contemporary bioethics incredible will welcome its main contentions, practitioners and followers of bioethics will dismiss those contentions. I hope this is not altogether so. The reasoning in the first half of Chapter 3 directly engages with the arguments of the bioethicists. Their case for dismissing what we customarily say about the killing of infants, the demented and the disabled is replied to in terms which should not be unfamiliar to them. The methods of argument and reflection employed in the latter half of the chapter are indeed alien to contemporary practical ethics and may thus pass its practitioners by.

There is a governing thought implicit in much of this book which does indeed mark its approach as being different from that of much of contemporary applied moral philosophy, this being the thought that issues in the moral life cannot be solved by the production of yet more sophisticated theories. The problems explored in the book raise fundamental questions about our thought of ourselves as human beings, about equality, about justice and the like. In saying that the attempt to mediate between the perceptions of a parent and of a philosopher is a failure, I witness to my sense that I have as yet no fully satisfactory answers to these questions, indeed am not altogether sure how answers to them may be arrived at. There are matters here beyond my present understanding. This point is also reflected in the tentative, exploratory character of the contents of Chapter 4 on infanticide and abortion and of the treatment of justice in Chapter 5. At the end of Chapter 6 readers will find a brief summary of Charles Taylor's thoughts on the 'ethics of inarticulacy'. This book's limited ability to be fully articulate about the fundamental values it invokes is a consequence of a sense that to be too fully or easily articulate on the matters broached in it will be to falsify our perceptions. The strictures, in that chapter, on the attempt to solve problems about the morality of action and policy toward the mental handicapped by slapping theological theories on to the table is another reflection of its sense of the consequences of too easy an articulacy.

What I have done in this Preface is provide a defence of murk in moral philosophy and I should stop before that scandalous procedure goes any further.

A note on terminology

There are many ways of referring to those of our fellow human beings who are impaired in mental functions, including 'mentally handi-capped', 'mentally deficient', 'mentally retarded', 'person with learning difficulties'. I address the matter of how to pick out this class of human beings in Chapter 2 and argue there in favour of my own usage: 'cog-nitively disabled'. Prior to that point, I use 'mentally handicapped' for the simple reason that it is the phrase which has been most current in British English.

A note on references

References to books and articles are given in endnotes to the chapters and printed at the close of the book. Short titles are given in the Notes, titles being spelt out in the Bibliography after the Notes.

Acknowledgements

I am greatly indebted to Mark Wynn for reading the entirety of this book in draft. He provided numerous suggestions for improving the text, many of which I have shamelessly incorporated without acknowledgement. The publisher's reader also offered me a series of challenging and acute criticisms.

1
The Philosophical Problem

Philosophical doubts about the personhood of the mentally handicapped

Philosophical scepticism about the personhood of the mentally handicapped can be found explicit or implicit in a wide range of recent moral philosophy. As noted in the Preface, such scepticism frequently starts from consideration of how, if at all, we may justify the different treatment Western societies have meted out to animals and human beings. Consider the conduct of medical and scientific research.

In medical and biological research we do the following kinds of things to animals: we breed them specially for this purpose; we deprive them of their liberties, keeping them caged in laboratories; we introduce them to harmful diseases and agents; we modify their normal genetic structures so that they grow up deficient in basic attributes of their kind; we kill them in order to harvest the data arising out of our manipulations of them. We would not customarily think that any such practices would be appropriate for human beings. When practices of this kind have been directed to human beings, as they were by Nazi and Japanese doctors in World War II, they have been condemned by humanity at large. Again, we breed animals for captivity and death in the meat and livestock industry. The jokes of a Jonathan Swift apart, no one would think this appropriate for human beings.

If such discriminating practices cannot be justified, then they ought to stop. Proponents of vegetarianism, veganism and ecological consciousness cannot find the discriminating practices justified and heroically accept the consequences.[1] Many would think such a policy heroic, if only because they would regard the use of animal subjects in biomedical research as of vital importance.[2] Such a stance demands that

1

something be found which shows that human beings and animals deserve difference of treatment, that the moral status of human beings is appropriately different from that of animals. Two constraints now enter into the way in which recent moral philosophy has developed the argument from this point. They are, first, that the feature (or set of features) which demonstrates difference of moral status cannot be the mere fact that human beings are human and animals are not, and second, that whatever the feature is it must be empirically discernible (discernibly present in human beings and discernibly absent in animals).

We cannot take the mere fact that someone is a human being as a reason for giving them a moral status different from animals, on the ground that to do so would fall into the trap of speciesism. Speciesism is defined as giving human life a special priority because it is human.[3] This is deemed to be analogous to racism, in that it treats people, or beings, of a certain group differently from those of other groups solely on the grounds of group membership and not on account of any relevant, discernible differences between individual members of these groups.

The constraint which tells us that only empirically discernible facts about human beings can properly ground an affirmation of enhanced moral status reflects a requirement that moral claims as important as those under consideration should be the subject of proper public debate and checking. Unlike affirmations of personal preference, moral claims have, paradigmatically, a claim upon all. If something is a genuine moral value, it should be capable of being commended to, and being recognised by, everyone. Such commendation and recommendation is in turn possible only if three interlocking conditions are met: moral claims must be supported by impersonal reasons; they must not depend directly upon personal feelings; and they must be subject to empirical confirmation.[4] These conditions imply that any qualities held to justify the assertion that human beings have a special moral status should be publicly discernible. Hence, it cannot be that we need to be adherents of some religion or other to note their presence. It cannot be that we need to be in receipt of some revelation or other to be aware of them. This means that a 'property' such as 'being made in God's image' cannot be one that in and of itself establishes the distinct moral status of human beings, since we have to subscribe to a particular religion and revelation to discern such a thing. The argument about the empirically checkable character of any affirmation of the worth of humans is meant by its proponents to rule out all appeals to theology as a solution to our problems in this field.[5] An extended discussion of the role theological reflection might play in the ethics of mental handicap will be given in Chapter 6. Let us accept for the sake of the argument which leads up to that chapter that we do have a reason for ignoring theological claims in this area.

The one discernible property which sets human beings apart from other creatures and which seems to be relevant to the moral issues involved is intelligence and what flows from its possession: self-consciousness, autonomy and rationality. What interests philosophers in particular is the ability of normal, adult human beings to refer their experiences and desires to a sense of themselves as agents and subjects who endure through time. Normal human beings are not creatures who merely have experiences and desires. They are creatures who can accompany those things with a sense of self and can refer to items of consciousness as things which they have. Human beings can give substantive content to the idea of themselves as having these thoughts, these desires because they can recall past thoughts and preferences and project themselves into the future. Human beings can place themselves in the past and in the future as having done this or that or as possibly going to do this or that. The ability so to place one's thoughts and desires is a reflection of the human being's possession of language. The human being can recall events removed from the present and contemplate future possibilities which are not given in any present stimulus. Consider: a dog may react with excitement to its owner's taking its lead down. 'It expects to go for a walk', we say. Here the future is present in a current stimulus. One could not say of a dog, as one could say of a human being, 'She expects to be doing so-and-so in the distant future'. In order to do that the human being has to be able to contemplate possibilities represented before the mind in the absence of some immediate stimulus. Only by means of language, or some equivalent symbolic system, can one represent possibilities not immediately present in some stimulus. The same applies to memory.

So: normal human beings are creatures with a language and they do not therefore live wholly in the present or in the immediate past and future. They have a sense of themselves as beings who endure. They can thus have reflective and long-term goals and desires. They are thus capable of genuine planning for the future, the kind of planning which entails deliberating with a view to forming conscious intentions, which may then be acted upon and followed through when circumstances obtain. None of this can be said to be true of animals for the reasons hinted at above (leaving aside, for now, the borderline cases of chimpanzees who have allegedly learnt American Sign Language). By way of clinching this point consider the example of consent to medical treatment. We accept that a human infant cannot give or withhold consent to a medical procedure. It may be able to show signs of aversion or pleasure at some proffered treatment, such as a drug. But it cannot understand what it is being proffered. It cannot envisage for itself two futures – one with and one without the course of treatment – and decide which future it prefers. The absence of language alone prevents it from doing any of this. For the same reason, an animal cannot consent or dissent from medical treatment or enrolment into a medical research programme, albeit that it, like the baby, can manifest signs of aversion or acceptance of what is happening to it.

Self-consciousness as we have described it brings in autonomy. Autonomy is a feature of the agency of those beings who can act on the basis of a reflective desire for the kind of future they want and for the kind of beings they want to be. An autonomous being is thus capable of providing, on the basis of these reflective desires, its own laws for its actions (hence, the name 'autonomous'). In particular, it is not bound to act merely out of the press of the present desire which is strongest, nor merely for the sake of plans provided for it by others. It can formulate its own conscious intents and purposes and act on them. It is capable of planning its own future and acting on those plans.

Autonomy as described above ushers in rationality. A being who was capable of reflection on its past, present and future, but who lacked the means of deciding on the merits of competing futures or the means of planning what to do in order to gain a desired future in the circumstances surrounding it, would not be truly autonomous. So an autonomous creature must be a rational creature, capable of contemplating reasons for action, deciding between them and acting upon them.

Self-consciousness, autonomy and rationality all involve and presuppose intelligence on the part of the creature who possesses them. Intelligence is entailed in the ability to master a language, which we have seen is essential if the autonomous being is to hold before it a past and future with any depth to them. To master the difference between past, present and future the self-conscious creature must be capable of taking evidence and signs in the present as revelatory of what happened in the past or as indicators of what may happen in the future. Such a being must be able to distinguish between those factors in present experience which are evidence for what happened in the past and those which point to what might happen in the future. But to be able to do that entails having general beliefs about the world, some of which must be reliable. The ability to form reliable general beliefs about the world depends on the possession of powers of memory, discrimination and reasoning which all reflect intelligence in their possessor.[6]

To sum up: the self-conscious, rational creature must live in a world which is more than an array of present stimuli. It must have some comprehension of this world as having a past and an array of possible futures. It is able to discern and comprehend its existence through this past and into those futures. Such general, non-specific knowledge is a product of intelligence. It is not given to the human infant but is acquired alongside massive intellectual development. If it is not present in animals, it is equally not present in many human beings, specifically: infants, the senile demented, the permanently comatose and perhaps some of the severely mentally handicapped.

We are well on our way now to seeing how the drive toward a mark of moral status that is not speciesist but is empirically discernible leads to a criterion of personhood which places a question mark, to say the least, over those human beings whose intellectual development is disordered or retarded and who may, in consequence, not acquire that sufficient grasp of language, self and the world which allows them to function as fully self-conscious, autonomous and rational creatures. We are moving away from Simone Weil's advocacy of equality based on respect for the human being as such.

The argument remains to be completed by reviewing how self-consciousness and the rest are deemed to make the decisive moral difference in recent, English-speaking moral philosophy. At the cost of some oversimplification, we can divide the kinds of moral outlook used to complete the argument about moral status into three types: pure utilitarianism, contractarianism and impure utilitarianism.

By a 'pure utilitarianism' is meant a moral outlook which remains true to the tenets that the worth of actions resides solely in their consequences and that morally relevant consequences consist in the creation of valued (or disvalued) experiences. So the pure utilitarian sees self-consciousness, autonomy and rationality as making the difference to the moral status of (most) human beings because they make possible rich kinds of experience, kinds of experience not possible for beings lacking these traits. A pure utilitarian defence of the enhanced moral status of beings with autonomy is mounted by Frey. He contends that 'autonomy is only instrumentally valuable'[7] but that its instrumental value is enormous. A being who is autonomous is capable of forming its own conception of the good life and of acting so as to realise that conception. Thus its life can be full of self-fulfilment and achievement and can be enriched in ways not at all possible for an animal. He writes of the value of a 'life of accomplishment'.[8] The experiences of an autonomous being are then much richer and more complex than those of a non-autonomous being. Beings who can live autonomous lives are more valuable morally speaking and therefore a greater wrong is done when such a being is killed. The wrongness is a function of the destruction of something of value.

In contrast to the utilitarian attempt to make matters of obligation a function of the promotion of valuable states of affairs, contemporary contractarian ethics sees them as the outcome of agreement and bargaining. Human beings in the typical case are creatures capable of autonomous, rational agency. They each have a unique set of preferences which defines their individual good. They need, however, the co-operation and non-interference of the other rational agents who make up the moral community if they are to have a chance of enacting their conception of the good. The principles of right are those which all such agents should assent to if they have in mind the creation of a social order which enables them as individuals to pursue their preferences. Given that individuals can only pursue their conception of the good with the co-operation and non-interference of others, they all have a reason to accept constraints upon their pursuit of satisfaction, constraints which establish conditions for such co-operation and non-interference. Only thus is everyone's liberty as an autonomous agent guaranteed. In this light, the basic moral rules forbidding murder, theft and the like and enjoining mutual aid can be seen as the outcome of a quasi-contract between all rational human beings: they accept some constraints on preference pursuit in order to ensure conditions of liberty and freedom from harm which make such pursuit overall possible.[9]

It is an important corollary of such contractarian accounts of the foundations of ethics that moral rules exist as the outcome of a quasi-agreement among autonomous agents and therefore exist in order to protect each such agent's vital interest in pursuing its own conception of the good in favourable circumstances. Agents who are not party to, and cannot be party to, the contract because they are not autonomous are not directly protected by it. In consequence, they cannot but have a lower moral status than autonomous agents. Morality being a function of those mutual interests in preference pursuit unique to autonomous agents, it cannot apply to those outside the terms of the contract. The conclusion is drawn by Gauthier: 'Animals, the unborn, the congenitally handicapped and defective fall beyond the pale of morality tied to mutuality'.[10] Such a view allows of a sharp distinction between the moral status of animals and human beings, as is noted by Rawls.[11] It seems to create a sharp division between the moral status of adults and children (or at least infants) since the latter are not autonomous agents to at all the same degree. This verdict on children can be avoided if the contractarian is allowed to argue that the *potentiality* for partnership in the moral contract is sufficient for enhanced moral status.[12] Appeal to potentiality still allows a distinction to be drawn between animals and humans which is empirically based.

The theoretical base of contractarian deductions of fundamental moral principles and rules is notably richer than that required for a simple utilitarianism. Not surprisingly, the mechanics of the contractarian deduction have come under heavy critical fire in the literature.[13] Many philosophical commentators on medical ethics employ an impure utilitarianism which mixes elements of utilitarianism with a contractarian emphasis on the intrinsic value of autonomy. On this view, the fundamental value of a life depends on its quality or richness, but independent weight is given to respect for autonomous creatures and their choices. This impure utilitarianism is shown in Jonathan Glover's account of the ethics of homicide, according to which two kinds of reason are allowed as legitimate objections to killing. One reason invokes a straightforwardly utilitarian value: 'the undesirability of shortening a worth-while life'. The other invokes 'the undesirability of overriding someone's autonomy'.[14] These two reasons provide conditions which are separately necessary for killing to be licit. It is wrong to kill if the consequential good of maximising the amount of worthwhile life (worthwhile in terms of its promotion of happiness for the individual) is thereby destroyed. Killing is also wrong if it is against the self-conscious desire of the victim for more life.

The need to introduce a non-utilitarian value into the determination of the worth of persons should be obvious. Without such a value it is difficult to gain a sense that a wrong is done to the *victim* in an act of unjustified homicide. It is difficult on a pure utilitarianism to avoid making trade-offs between killing one individual and saving others in order to maximise general utility. If people are so many units of potential utility one can balance increasing the welfare of many against the killing of some. Further, we may be hard pushed to distinguish the morality of a decision not to create possible people from the morality of a decision to destroy actual people. In short, we will be pressed to explain why we value the individual human being's existence and think the individual is owed justice or enjoys rights.[15]

Impure utilitarianism of this type allows the philosophical moralist to respect the modish desire to ground principles and rules of right on the appeal to the rights possessed by individuals. Respect for the value of autonomy is alleged to lie behind such appeals to rights. The resulting view is theoretically less tidy than either pure utilitarianism or contractarianism. Both of these views depend on clear metaphysical outlooks on the nature and value of human beings. Pure utilitarianism sees value in states of mind or the satisfaction of preferences and regards human beings as the sites of such value. They are richer sites than animals and are to be treated differently in accordance with that fact, but the difference remains one of degree rather than kind. Contractarianism fits into a view derived from a reading of Kantian ethics which sees value as residing in rational agency as such. Human beings (or most of them) are uniquely valuable because they are the only instances of such agency we know. Impure utilitarianism of Glover's kind does not tie into a coherent metaphysics in the same way. Its defence is that its fundamental moral principles best cohere with our reflective moral judgements on matters to do with the treatment of human beings. One of the underlying issues aired in this study is how far we can or must have an ethics devoid of backing by a metaphysics. I shall suggest as the argument unfolds that we can have such an ethics, but, unlike the impure utilitarian, only if we stick much more closely to the pattern of ordinary moral judgement.

The issues in moral theory raised immediately above deserve much greater attention than I can give them now. They will surface again in Chapters 3 and 6. At this point we must note that the three moral outlooks appear to agree on the point that human beings incapable of self-conscious, autonomous existence are of less value than those who are so capable. These outlooks therefore pose a question about the worth of the lives of the mentally handicapped and the extent to which we owe such folk the normal obligations of justice and aid. The threat to the status of the mentally handicapped as persons arises both directly and indirectly from this philosophical consensus.

Some philosophers sharing the above consensus deduce the non-personhood of the mentally handicapped directly from the philosophical consensus on personhood. James Rachels in his *The End of Life* distinguishes between 'being alive' and 'having a life' in the sense of having a biography.[16] A dog merely has a life; a normal human being has a biographical life because its existence is infused with the qualities we have described under the heading of self-consciousness, autonomy and rationality. He invites us to compare the harm in the death of two people: one 'seriously retarded' and the other normal. The death of the former is less tragic than the death of the latter because less can be said about why the death of the seriously retarded person is a bad thing. In just the same way we can say less about why the death of a dog is a bad thing.[17] Of a baby born with massive handicaps and with a very poor prognosis, Rachels says that, since she will never have a biographical life, 'there is nothing to be concerned with, from a moral point of view'.[18]

Rachels' views hint at a sliding scale of value. The more mentally handicapped people are, the less they count as persons, as having lives worth preserving and the less normal rules surrounding homicide apply to them. A rational account can be given of why having a life is of value. Normal human beings are complex creatures who have a rich mixture of desires, who can enjoy pleasure and pain, manifest curiosity, form friendships and so forth. The presence of such things in a life makes that life of value to its possessor. A life is of value if it contains such positive elements. It follows that if we subtract the positive elements the value will be diminished.[19] Hence, the value of the lives of the mentally handicapped must be diminished to the extent that their lives cannot contain Rachels' positive elements. Frey states a very similar view in a number of papers. Frey is exercised by the question of how, if at all, we can deem the use of animals in harmful, lethal medical experiments licit while deeming the use of human beings in similar experiments illicit. We have noted already that Frey thinks that the value of a human life does not depend on its being human, but on its richness, which is a function of the possession of autonomy. This leads him to the following 'position on vivisection':

> Experimentation on animals for human benefit is nearly always justified by the appeal to the difference in value between their lives; but the lives of some humans are of a quality comparable to or even below that of many of the healthy animals on whom the experiments are performed. Why, then, not perform the experiments on humans? The benefit to be derived could be equally, if not better, obtained, since often the extrapolation of results from animal to human cases is not very reliable.[20]

Whom does he have in mind as human candidates for vivisection? Avoiding what he describes as the 'temptation' to select the irreversibly comatose, he begins a list which starts with the 'very severely mentally enfeebled, the seriously brain damaged, severely handicapped new-borns'.[21] So it is clear that the mentally handicapped are the first candidates. Frey acknowledges that there may be a utilitarian argument from side effects to bar human experiments, a case centring upon the outrage caused by his proposal. His response is to appeal to the possibility that such feelings of outrage may be 'susceptible to removal by education, information and careful explanation of the arguments'.[22] He is in effect asserting here that the negative value of outraged feelings is a product of ignorant, non-philosophically informed sentiments within the moral community. Train its members in moral philosophy well enough and the feelings will not arise.

The direct attack on the moral status of the mentally handicapped is to be seen in the creation of a sliding scale of personhood and value determined by the presence or lack of self-consciousness, autonomy and rationality. Those with a mental handicap of such a severe kind as to throw doubt on their possession of these value-making qualities slide to the bottom of the scale. When they are judged to reach that point, their lives are of no more significance than the lives of animals. They can then be treated accordingly. They are not to be treated like human beings and the protection we enjoy from principles of justice and mutual aid is not to be afforded them. They are to be expelled from the moral community.

We are confronting the reasoned, philosophical justification of the idea of a sliding scale of moral worth, a scale determined ultimately by intelligence and intellectual development (for, as noted above, these are the basis for the possession of self-consciousness, autonomy and reason). The promotion and application of the sliding scale of moral worth offers a powerful threat to the very severely handicapped and a lesser threat to all mentally retarded people. Even though many of the mentally handicapped, even the majority (see the next chapter), develop into self-conscious beings, any equation in the public consciousness between moral worth and the development of intelligence will have deleterious consequences for them. There is a more potent threat to *all* mentally handicapped people in the indirect result of the philosophical consensus described in this section. The result in question is the endorsement the consensus provides for infanticide. Once it becomes accepted that killing a human infant is somehow less heinous, less deserving of the description 'murder', than killing an adult human being, the future existence of a population of mentally handicapped people in the human community will be seen as a grave error to be avoided. The mentally handicapped adults amongst us will be seen as people who should have been killed in infancy.

The apology for infanticide undertaken by many contemporary moral philosophers develops from the analysis of moral status and moral personhood outlined above. Since babies and infants lack self-consciousness and all that is associated with it, then they are not moral persons. They are not protected by the rules of justice (or: are not the possessors of rights). Glover sums up the movement of thought involved by noting that 'the direct objections to infanticide are relatively weak'.[23] To the account of moral worth outlined in this section, Glover need only add a dismissal of the defence that infants are *potential* persons and therefore should be treated like *actual* persons. The dismissal is grounded on the thought that considering that something is potentially a person no more makes it one than noting that a cake can be made from the ingredients in front of you makes those ingredients into an actual cake.[24] For someone like Glover, the wrongness of infanticide lies in its side effects, specifically the distress and outrage it causes to those adults affected by it and the reduction it may occasion in the number of future worthwhile lives.[25] On Glover's impure utilitarianism, once the bar of violating autonomy is shown not to be present, only consequential considerations could decide the matter. Glover here speaks for a consensus on the morality of infanticide amongst a significant group of contemporary moral philosophers, as can be established by reading such books as Kuhse and Singer's *Should the Baby Live?*, Rachels' *The End of Life* and Tooley's *Abortion and Infanticide*.

Now many, including myself, will consider such views abhorrent and totally unacceptable because of the general licence they give to the killing of human babies. However, I wish to set aside such a response in order to focus on the particularly grave threat to the mentally handicapped which arises out of these philosophical arguments. Once considerations of utility and expediency become the only relevant ones governing the treatment of babies and infants diagnosed as likely to have significant mental handicaps, then it is mandatory to look at whether the side effects involved in killing the infant are outweighed by the benefit of avoiding the distresses and costs entailed by letting the child live and grow to be handicapped. Once more, Glover provides a succinct summary of the point:

> Where the handicap is sufficiently serious, the killing of a baby may benefit the family to an extent that is sufficient to outweigh the unpleasantness of the killing (or the slower process of 'not striving to keep alive').[26]

Glover's conclusions on the licitness of killing the new-born handicapped are matched by statements in other examples of the philosophical literature cited in this section. The seriousness of the threat they represent can be seen fully when we take note both of the way in which such conclusions can be extended by other philosophers and of the manner in which such philosophising meshes in with developments in contemporary clinical practice.

Let us first consider how Glover's conclusion is extended by some philosophers. Once it is accepted that self-consciousness, autonomy and rationality provide the decisive threshold for a principled objection to killing and that no appeal to the potential of something to display these properties is allowed, then only consideration of side effects and consequences becomes important in deciding on the licitness of killing. The fact that a baby who is handicapped may grow into an adult nonetheless capable of displaying the threshold qualities is not decisive. For the mere fact of handicap will entail that vast additional negative utilities attach to nurturing that child, negative utilities not attached to nurturing a normal child. It will then be asked whether the expected later quality of life of the child and its contributions to the human community outweigh the costs involved in its nurture (and indeed in any support it will require as an adult). Recall that no wrong can be done to the baby about whose future these judgements are being made because, like all babies, it is below the threshold where notions of wronging someone gain a purchase. A simple estimate of expected, net utilities is in order. Thus, for example, we find Kuhse and Singer pleading that we should take into account the economic costs of letting babies live who are diagnosed as likely to be handicapped. They point with alarm to the alleged increase in the number of mentally (and physically) handicapped people consequent on improvements in gynaecological and paediatric medicine. They urge us to accept that the moneys devoted to the mentally handicapped will be better spent elsewhere.[27] For the reasons outlined above, such arguments can be mounted regardless of whether those babies diagnosed as mentally handicapped can or cannot be expected to cross the magic threshold of philosophical personhood if they are allowed to live and become adults. What Kuhse and Singer are in effect doing is arguing that a rational society should cull babies and infants according to calculations of net utility centring on the degree of intellectual and physical normality they can be expected to have in the future. This is tantamount to giving the following message to the many mentally handicapped people who can perfectly well understand it: if things had been properly ordered in our communities, and if we had possessed sufficient predictive expertise, you should have been culled in infancy. The existence of such folk is a mistake, one whose repetition can be avoided for the future if we return to the morality of the Greeks and Romans (who sent unwanted babies to their deaths) and forget that of Christianity.[28]

The theorising of moral philosophers may seem harmless enough were it not for the fact that such reasoning about the handicapped is reflected in aspects of clinical practice. Indeed, the worlds of contemporary medicine and moral philosophy now interconnect, thanks to the rise of bioethics. Hence, it is quite likely that strands of paediatric practice toward the handicapped new-born have been buttressed by, even while not originating in, moral philosophy of the type explored here. It is a fact that the medical literature contains many examples of papers describing and advocating the selective non-treatment of new-borns based on judgements as to the expected degree of future handicaps.[29] The existence of such policies in paediatric medicine has also come to public consciousness through celebrated legal cases in a range of Western countries (the 'Arthur case' will figure as an example in Chapter 4 below). To an extent which I cannot determine, our society has unsystematically and unintentionally embarked on the eugenic policies advocated by some moral philosophers.

Philosophers who comment on the existence and nature of mentally handicapped people display no great awareness of who these people are, of the vast differences between them in the way of attainment and of the many possibilities of fulfilment available to them.[30] Philosophers have proffered a stipulative definition of 'person' which ties personhood to self-consciousness, autonomy and rationality. A special category of human beings is thus carved out: human beings who are not persons. The direct threat to the personal status of those profoundly handicapped individuals who may not cross the philosopher's threshold should call for the most careful description of who might fall into this rejected class and for a precise account of the respects on which their abilities leave them below the threshold. Philosophers of personhood are not directly interested in the ethical and social issues surrounding the status of the adult mentally handicapped. They are directly interested in commenting on and reforming practices toward babies and infants (bizarre though the direction of their interest might appear to most of us). They are also interested in our treatment of animals, and specifically in nailing the evils of speciesism. I have shown how their interest in paediatric medicine does not require these writers to establish whether infants with a prognosis of future handicap would or would not fall below the threshold of personhood offered by these moral philosophers. It is enough that we accept that future handicap entails some large degree of cost (to parents, carers and society at large) in order for the eugenic argument to seem plausible. In a parallel way, a vague reference to the 'seriously retarded' or those with 'profound deficit' is enough to establish that there are at least some human beings (who and how many does not matter) who are no higher than some animals in the way of intellectual attainments. Such a vague conclusion suffices to launch an argument of this kind: 'We must be inconsistent if we will not let *any* human being be used as a laboratory subject but will let *any* animal, regardless of whether it is a rat or one of the higher apes, be so used'.

As noted above, many will properly reject the intellectual moves documented in this section as morally and intellectually irresponsible on the simple yet powerful ground that they entail outrageous conclusions about human infants. Once more, I wish to focus on a further element of apparent irresponsibility in their implications for mentally handicapped persons. Assertions are being made about fellow human beings which denigrate them in the absence of any attempt to specify to whom the assertions apply and why. There is a further tendency in such writing to charge in the vaguest way that some fellow human beings are getting consideration and care which they do not deserve and which is better deserved by some animals. The philosophers cited on the subject of research ethics are in effect making this very point. The point is plain in Rachels' comment on the expected result of comparing creatures on the basis of the complexity of their lives: 'there would be reason to prefer the life of the animal to that of the human'.[31]

The exclusion of some of us from the human community needs to be resisted. Simone Weil's plea for equality needs to be defended with the mentally handicapped specifically in mind.

The theological interest

The final chapter of this work looks at theological issues surrounding mental handicap. This is not just because of my professional interests as a philosopher of religion. Theology is relevant to the pros and cons of the debate between defenders of customary morality and the common law, on the one hand, and contemporary moral philosophy, on the other. We have seen that the drive to establish certain attainments based on intelligence and development as the criteria of moral worth rests on the alleged necessity to rest moral worth on empirically manifest properties of human beings. But any such set of properties is always likely to be present in only some human beings. Human beings are different from one another. Some just do have profound deficit and delayed development when compared with the majority.

So we might be tempted to accept the following conclusion: if we adopt an empirically discernible quality (or qualities) as the basis for moral worth, our resulting criterion is bound to be discriminatory. If, by contrast, we want a criterion which is non-discriminatory and which grounds a universal moral respect for human beings, that on which the criterion is based cannot be an empirical quality. Perhaps we need a spiritual or religious quality or dimension to the human, such as our all sharing 'the image of God'. So, we will be driven into the horns of the following uncomfortable dilemma: either we accept a theological (or religious or revealed) basis for the ascription of fundamental worth to all human beings, or we follow the likes of Frey, Glover and Rachels and discriminate among human beings.

The incipient charge is that the authors described in this chapter are showing where a consistent secularism must lead. Since secularism leads to something decent people must regard as horrendous, reflection on the moral status of the mentally handicapped provides a moral argument for the truth of some brand of religious metaphysics.[32] You cannot have Simone Weil's ethics without her theology.

Thus we see how there is a deep theological, religious issue at the heart of the discussion of the ethics of mental handicap. We also see that secular and theological moralists frequently espouse the same critical principle when it comes to determining how we are to treat human beings. This is the principle that giving human beings the protection of customary rules of homicide and the like depends on showing that they have some property *over and above their being human* which makes them worthy of that protection. The disagreement between the secular and the theological moralists rests upon what property we are to select in order to meet the terms of the principle.

2
Defining Mental Handicap

Definitional issues

Anyone who has explored the literature on mental handicap will realise very quickly that there is a live issue as to whether and how a category of mentally handicapped people can be delineated. We may divide the questions this issue poses into substantive and terminological ones. It is a substantive question as to whether there is a worthwhile distinction of any kind to be made between the cognitively normal and the cognitively disabled. Even those who agree that there is a worthwhile distinction can then disagree about further substantive issues, such as the precise basis on which the distinction can be drawn and on whether, within this class of the disabled, there are further important demarcations to make (as between, for example, socio-cultural mental handicap and clinical handicap). We find terminological questions attached to these debates about matters of substance. If it is accepted that there is a distinction between the mentally handicapped and the normal and a clear notion of the mentally handicapped to go with it, we may still confront arguments about what are the correct terms to mark the distinction and to refer to the category of folk thus created.

The substantive questions concerning the demarcation of the category of the mentally handicapped will be dealt with in two separate discussions within this study. This chapter will tackle those substantive problems surrounding the category, which can be styled 'conceptual', or 'scientific'. Such problems centre on the claim that there is no reasoned basis on which to make the distinction and on the further claim that no scientific precision can be given to any contrast we might want to draw between the handicapped and the normal in respect of intelligence and mental functioning. In Chapter 5 we shall deal with the separate but related question of the political and ethical import of such a distinction. We shall consider arguments to the effect that the distinction is one element of a system of oppression towards those people society would label as mentally handicapped, retarded or the like. The case to be considered in that chapter is that the distinction is untenable because of its socio-political consequences. The socio-political critique of the notion of mental handicap might build upon any verdict that the distinction between mentally handicapped and normal was untenable on theoretical grounds. If the distinction is scientifically or philosophically unsound, the alleged fact that it was the agent of oppression would help explain its prevalence and grip. However, even if the distinction is judged to be theoretically sound, some will still urge that its public use be abandoned because it serves harmful ends.

Let us first turn though to matters strictly terminological and ask what terms we should use in endeavouring to frame a distinction between the normal and the mentally handicapped.

Thus far I have employed the phrase 'mentally handicapped' because it is the one most familiar to British ears. In North America 'mentally retarded' and 'mentally deficient' appear to be more current. There is a strong argument against pursuing clarity via the label of 'mental handicap'. The notion of a handicap is in large measure relational. I am long-sighted and find it very difficult to make out small objects close to. The extent to which this impairment in me is handicapping depends first on my job. Given that my work entails a great deal of reading, significant handicap looms. However, technology and wealth in my society makes excellent reading glasses easily available and the degree of handicap I face is insignificant. So whether, and to what degree, a condition of a person is handicapping is a function not just of facts about them but about their circumstances. Describing people as 'mentally handicapped' is not directly and exclusively describing them. If they are handicapped by impairments in cognitive function that will be a fact arising out of the relation between their impairments and their circumstances. The term 'handicapped' should therefore be avoided if the aim is to pick out something about a class of people that genuinely makes them different.

The World Health Organisation's distinction between disability and handicap is helpful in this context. The WHO defines disability as 'any restriction or lack (resulting from an impairment) of ability to perform an activity in the manner or within the range considered to be normal for a human being. Handicap is the resulting personal and social disadvantage.'[1] A disability, based on an impairment, can be handicapping or not depending both on the severity of the disability but crucially also on the nature of the disabled person's surroundings. The WHO defines impairment as the loss of, or abnormality in, structure or function.[2] This definition is obviously meant to enable impairments to serve as that on which disabilities are grounded. My lack of ability to see small print is grounded on an impairment in the muscles controlling the focusing of the eyes. We may think of the disability as primarily the property of the person, the impairment on which it rests as primarily the property of a part or subsystem of the person. We might say of the person that s/he has a disability, but of a part or subsystem of the person that it is impaired.

Some immediate issues arising out of the disability/handicap distinction need to be noted. First, the dependence of the fact and degree of handicap upon the surroundings of a person with disability allows room to argue that the fact of handicap is entirely a result of social attitudes, so that the category of 'the handicapped' is through and through socially constructed. This argument will be examined in Chapter 5. Second, we note that the notion of disability still contains a relational element. Its sense depends upon a notion of normal functioning and in what follows we will have to weigh the claims of those who contend that such a reference to the normal is intellectually and morally untenable. Third, we should be wary of swift attempts to banish the notion of handicap (or the handicapped) from our thinking altogether. David Pailin, for example, contends that the label presupposes that human life is a competition, in which, like racehorses perhaps, some carry a disadvantage imposed upon them. Since the view of life as a competition is untenable, if not vicious in its consequences, so is the notion of people possessing handicaps.[3] In reply, it must be stated that all that is needed for the notion of handicap to gain a purchase is the thought that people are goal-directed animals. They seek ends. They have to do things if they are to survive and flourish. They can be handicapped (disadvantaged) in doing and achieving things by virtue of disabilities and impairments.

It looks as though an initial terminology for our subject matter should speak of disablement rather than handicap, because of the radically relational character of the notion of handicap. 'Mentally disabled' is not quite right in my view because 'mental' is too broad in its implications. It implies disability/impairment across the entire spectrum of a person's non-physical life. 'Intellectually disabled' is too narrow, for it bids us focus on a lack of cleverness or intelligence as the decisive factor, whereas the example of conditions like autism will be seen to bring in something different from a lack of intelligence. For these reasons I prefer 'cognitively disabled' and 'cognitive disability' to refer to a lack of capacity to learn and understand, implying deficits in many areas dependent upon understanding, such as the ability to reason, plan and relate to others. Henceforth, when I am not quoting or reporting others' words, I shall speak of the problems arising from cognitive disability.

It cannot be said that the arguments for this usage are conclusive. Readers should be warned that this usage is peculiar to this study. They can judge its adequacy by reference to what follows. They should also note my self-conscious departure from the current vogue for the phrases 'learning difficulty' and 'learning disability'. There are two reasons for their popularity as alternatives to 'mental handicap' and 'mental retardation' which can initially be noted. One is that they are felt to be less stigmatising and derogatory. Another is that in the education systems of countries such as the UK and the USA a global classification of children into those who are cognitively disabled and those who are not has rightly been seen to be fruitless. Rather, best practice now concentrates on the particular problems of the individual child who has difficulties with learning, of whatever type and however caused. Appropriate syllabus and placement is then a function of such individualised assessment. Types of learning difficulty can be classified and grouped together, but 'cognitive disability' and phrases of like meaning have proved too coarse-grained by far for such classification, even when qualified by gradations such as 'mild', 'moderate', 'severe' or 'profound'.

We can accept that the educational terminology and classification is appropriate in its home context without accepting its use in all contexts. An advantage of 'learning difficulty/disability' is that, if 'learning' is understood broadly enough, these phrases will focus our attention on the fact that cognitive disability has as its chief manifestation a failure to develop through acquiring intellectual, linguistic and social skills as members of the species normally do. 'Difficulty' also helps in suggesting that cognitive disability can be overcome in some degree through appropriate care and education and thus offers an incentive not to write off such people. A minor problem with 'learning difficulty/ disability' is that in some uses in educational psychology it refers specifically to problems in learning *not* produced by general cognitive disability, for example problems such as dyslexia.[4] A more serious objection to universal use of 'person with learning difficulties' to pick out what used to be called 'the mentally handicapped' is that this terminology might hide the full reality of cognitive disablement. Suppose you have an autistic son who reaches school age with a vocabulary measured in units of ten and a grasp of grammar extending at best to simple two-word phrases (for example, 'mo din' = 'more drink'). He thus has virtually no functioning language. Imagine he has behavioural problems to match. To say that this child has learning difficulties will tend to direct our attention on how he will cope with schooling. This child will certainly have difficulties in learning, in that narrower understanding of 'learning', but that is hardly the most obvious fact about him. The difficulties he faces now and throughout his life will show in all manner of contexts beyond the educational. There will be valid purposes of classification and description which entail that he is not to be classed with a child who is dyslexic or who has an attention deficit. For one thing, we might want to say that the child has learning difficulties because he has problems in cognition and delays in development which affect his global functioning.

Is there a category of the cognitively disabled?

There is no question that there are persons with global cognitive impairments, such as the autistic child described above. Here is another example:

> Vicky is 12½ and profoundly handicapped, with a mental age of about five months. She is doubly incontinent, bottle-fed and can only eat minced food. She is unable to play with toys or sit up without back support. . . .[5]

Here we are faced with a profound arrest of the normal processes of cognitive development in a child, to the point where awareness of, and control over, basic bodily functions such as posture is lacking. From the fact that such cases exist it does not follow that it is useful to employ the label 'cognitively disabled' to help pick them out. It may be that there is no general class of folk properly so described or that there is no reliable distinction to be made between this putative class and the class of so-called normal people.

There are at least two contexts in which the need for a class of the cognitively disabled, and for the associated distinction between that class and the normal, might arise. They are the social and the scientific. Let us concentrate on the social for the time being.

A wide variety of social concerns and desiderata can lead a community to notice that some of its members are cognitively disabled. Ashton and Ward list factors by which modern industrialised societies make the distinction. Society can recognise people in its midst who: have impaired or incomplete intellectual development; do not develop or learn as quickly as others; have a limited ability to learn and to put learning to use; have a limited capacity in speech, reading, writing and arithmetic; have difficulty in acquiring social skills. A society such as ours may notice that people can have these impairments permanently and thus distinguish such folk from those who are mentally ill.[6] The lack of, or deficit in, the array of skills described can be evident in many contexts. They may be noted in the family and in normal rearing, as is the case with Vicky. They may be noticed in schooling as with delay in reading and the like. They may be apparent in legal and quasi-legal contexts. For example, we may wonder if someone understands enough to make a contract and be bound by its terms. A court may enquire as to whether a potential witness has enough comprehension to be a reliable reporter of facts and to understand what it is to give evidence under oath. Deficiencies in cognitive ability may come to light in employment.

The existence of people picked out as possessing the multiple impairments described above may bring them to the attention of the state in a modern industrialised society. Depending upon their degree of disability, the parents of such individuals made need state-directed aid in bringing them up. These individuals may need special school arrangements. They may need training targeted at their disabilities after school age. They may be unable to look after themselves in adult life. They thus may require special forms of housing or work in adulthood. These points amount to a case for saying that there is utility in a social or administratively defined class of the cognitively disabled. However, it must be conceded that any such class defined for social or administrative purposes is shifting and vague. It is so, because many individuals in the putative class of the cognitively disabled who need state aid and social support in one context will not need it in others. For example, it is a well-documented fact that many people diagnosed in their childhood as cognitively disabled by the school system become 'administratively invisible' after leaving school. This is because, despite their profound scholastic limitations, they are able to function independently in social life and, at least in times of high employment, to get work.[7]

Hence, on a purely social-administrative criterion we may have to say that the incidence of cognitive disability fell through advancing age groups. Ashton and Ward note that English and Scottish law both give different statutory definitions of the equivalent of 'cognitively disabled' in different legal contexts because the needs and concerns of different statutes diverge.[8] No doubt other legal systems besides these two show the same pattern. With different aims in view, the law may thus alter the boundaries of the class from occasion to occasion. As against this, we should note that there are some people whose cognitive disabilities are profound enough to mean that they will be picked out as special by all the state's agencies and require social assistance of one kind or another throughout their lives.

Social-administrative criteria look as though they make a category of the cognitively disabled inevitable but vague and shifting, like the category of baldness. There are lots of men with bald pates to be seen, but there is no one single way of being bald and there is a large penumbra surrounding the distinction between those who are bald and those who are not.

Some may wish to go further. They may argue that the notion of the cognitively disabled is wholly culture relative and in fact a creation of the impact of modernity on Western societies. One can tell a story of the following kind. In pre-industrialised communities, and particularly in communities without a requirement for mass, formal education, a much greater tolerance of intellectual variability existed. With industrialisation, very much fewer people could work from and around the home. Factory work placed a premium on a narrower yet more demanding range of skills and required geographical mobility from the workforce. It prevented people working according to their own pace. By contrast, life in rural communities allowed many forms of relaxed styles of work. As industrialisation advanced, a literate and numerate working population was required. Tolerance for the slow learning decreased further. So it is our type of society which has created the need for a category of the cognitively disabled and also the need for state aid to look after the slow learning. In days past, they could be integrated into rural communities more easily and without the need for special support from outside the family or the village.

There is a grain of truth in the above picture, to the extent that those we label cognitively disabled often come to our notice through the school system. But the extent to which it is solely the demands of formal schooling in literacy and numeracy which create a category of the

cognitively disabled is limited. Many members of the admittedly heterogeneous group we are considering have problems in cognition which
are evident prior to schooling and continue long after. Moreover, there
is evidence, provided by the pioneering surveys of Robert Edgerton, to
the effect that all types of society, past and present, have recognised the
existence of cognitively disabled people.[9] Edgerton shows how studies
of non-technologically advanced societies have revealed that they have
words and practices marking out those among them who are cognitively
disabled. Stupidity and intelligence are matters of concern in hunter-
gatherer, herding and crop-growing communities. They are so because
human life is not easy. Skills are required to get food. All human lan-
guages are everywhere grammatically complex and rich in vocabulary.
Many forms of culture require good memory and skills in learning.
Human social life is everywhere complex and requires manifold skills
to master. The existence of people who find difficulty in learning, in
mastering language and in thinking is noted universally. Moreover,
Edgerton affirms on the basis of anthropological evidence he surveys
that, in the great majority of societies of which we know, the cognitively disabled are 'problem engendering'.[10] There are problems fitting
them into patterns of social living and work and they may need special
assistance and help. Those 'who learn slowly, plan poorly, remember
too little or solve problems incorrectly'[11] will create difficulties for many
social systems. Amateur evolutionary reflections support the idea that
we are here looking at a cultural universal. What has enabled *homo
sapiens* to survive is its ability to live in groups and defeat hostile and
harsh environments through intelligence and high levels of adaptabil-
ity. It has been of immeasurable help to the species that language and
culture have enabled later generations to store up the solutions of earlier
ones to problems of survival and allowed them to learn from their fore-
bears' mistakes. Intelligence, therefore, is likely to be a widespread
human trait and lack of it is also likely to be noted. In addition, the
universality of some forms of cognitive disability is guaranteed through
their grounding in forms of organic malfunction, as illustrated by fragile
X syndrome and Down's syndrome. Such syndromes can produce severe
forms of disability.

Edgerton does concede that there is no universal, cross-cultural
measure used to demarcate the cognitively disabled.[12] What precise
forms of deficiency in cognition are picked out as worthy of note in
one community will not be the same in all respects as those picked
out in another. That matter will vary as the needs and interests of

communities vary. So not all we classify as cognitively disabled will be so classified by others. Some members of our class would be invisible in other societies, and vice versa.

Even if the above argument about the trans-cultural viability of a category of the cognitively disabled is accepted, it is still open for someone to argue that there is something fundamentally confused in the attempt to create such a category. As the WHO definitions of 'disability' and 'impairment' make clear, these concepts are normative. A disability is 'any restriction or lack (resulting from an impairment) of ability to perform an activity in the manner or within the range considered to be normal for a human being'. Judging that someone is cognitively disabled is judging them against a norm provided by the typical intellectual, social and linguistic skills of human beings and finding that they do not meet the norm set by what is typical, by what is true of the majority. It may be urged at this point that there is no way in which the ethics of categorising can be kept out of the argument, since the normative character of the label 'cognitively disabled' demonstrates that to use it is to make a value judgement about large numbers of people. One of Pailin's central complaints against the notion of the handicapped can equally be seen as an objection against the notion of 'disabled':

> It indicates that the person so described lacks something which the describer regards as important. . . . Individuals are different. To use standards which one group finds as important as a basis for judging all others may be an act of unjustified imperialism.[13]

Prior to this he castigates the 'fundamental error' of 'presuming there is an identifiable norm for human being which all must seek to satisfy and against which all must be judged'.[14]

Is the concept of the cognitively disabled transparently evaluative? The answer is 'Yes and No'. It is a concept which involves judging by reference to a norm, but it entails no evaluation of the worth of the people to which the norm is applied.[15] In order to employ the concept we need to accept that human beings are adaptively organised beings; it is as if they are made to a design plan. They have evolved so as to enable them to meet species-typical ends and goals. Their parts and sub-systems are likewise adaptively organised and oriented toward the realisation of species-typical ends. In short, there is a human species-being. For example, we can judge from examining typical cases that human beings are built to see and that their eyes are constructed so that sight is possible. Someone who is long-sighted like Byrne lacks, to that extent, an ability and has eyes which malfunction in part. The disability is minor and the loss of function relatively unimportant. But we can judge, again from empirical evidence, that functioning sight is important in evolutionary terms for the survival of the species and thus discern why the species' adaptive organisation is such as to enable the human being to see in the typical case. So someone who has little or no functioning sight lacks something typical of the human being as such, has a disability and a noteworthy loss of functioning. None of these judgements presuppose or entail a judgement of how valuable people who suffer from loss of sight are as people. The judgements about loss of sight involving disability are built on relatively plain facts about the adaptiveness and designedness of the species and its typical members. They do not prevent us welcoming the existence of blind and partially sighted members of our community. We know that they often have compensating abilities which they themselves and the sighted value highly. To say that those with little or no sight have a disability is not an expression of disapproval of them as people. It is a statement of the fact that they do not function as typical members of the species do because subsystems within them do not function as they are adapted and designed to do.

The use of a norm provided by typical functioning and the apparent designedness and adaptive structure of the human being is not the application of a majority preference or of a simple comparison between what the majority can do and what a minority cannot do. It is conceivable that the majority of human beings become partially sighted or blind in the future. That situation could still be judged as the acquisition by the majority of a disability, because it could be discerned that the majority lacked in full a function which the human organism is adapted to have. The majority would thus become atypical of the species and its design plan. By analogy, it may be that the majority of thermostats in the world's buildings cease to function properly. We could tell that this was so by reference to the norm of what thermostats are adapted to do. That the adaptation of thermostats can be judged from plans and results from conscious design does not affect the essence of this analogy.

The irrelevance of the preferences of the majority for judging the existence of disability can be seen by extending the example of the community of the blind. Imagine Byrne is born into a society in which the majority are blind or only partially sighted and in which those with good, near-normal sight get the worst jobs and are very low down the social pecking order. Byrne's sightedness is now a handicap in these circumstances, at least to the extent that it results in social and economic disadvantage. But it would be wrong to label Byrne as disabled (though he may lack whatever compensating abilities, say in touch and hearing, that the blind and partially sighted can develop). We would be imagining a situation in which a specific disability was prevalent and favoured. What was abnormal, and a loss or diminution of functioning, judged by reference to the adaptive design and structure of the human organism, would have become normal in the sense of 'shared by the majority' and 'socially prized'.

In applying the above reflections to the case of cognitive disability, we would have to accept as fact that we can judge certain basic cognitive abilities to be typical of the human, a judgement based on the adaptive character of the human being and its subsystems. These abilities would be fundamental skills in learning, memory and understanding which enable human beings to function as planning agents, as communicators with members of their kind, as beings able to acquire skills, adapt their behaviour to changing circumstances and so forth. So, we must think of there being cognitive functions typical of the human being as such which arise out of the evolutionary history of the species. 'Cognitive disability' is thus not primarily a label for the lack of something we, the majority, prize and reward. It is a loss of, or deficiency in, function typical of the species as such and reflecting its adaptive structure. It is of course true that many societies have stigmatised the cognitively disabled and regarded people who lack intelligence very negatively. But such evaluations are not presupposed by or entailed in the judgement that disability is present when there is a deficiency in, or lack of, fundamental cognitive skills necessary for the basics of rational existence and social functioning.

The analogy between cognitive disability and deficiency in a physical ability typical of the species, such as sight or locomotion, may be objected to on the ground that it is possible to judge in a clear-cut way from a person's functioning and from the character of the relevant limbs or organs whether s/he is blind or unable to walk. There is none of the vagueness and penumbra which surrounds the category of the cognitively disabled. However, this intended contrast may be over-drawn. Loss of sight, for example, is not an all or nothing affair. Many of those who are classed as blind have some sight. The question of when impairment of vision becomes bad enough to invoke the classification of someone as visually disabled is to a large extent an administrative one. There are legal definitions of blindness in many countries. The definitions relate to such questions as when a child with poor sight can and cannot be taught in the same way as its sighted peers or when special employment protection or social security provision is to be offered to those with little functioning sight. It is easy to see that the point at which a degree of poor sight becomes something which interferes with education, social functioning and work will be relative to a large extent. In societies without compulsory, formal education or social security systems deciding when poor sight is to be classed as blindness will not arise in the same way as in ours. Different patterns of food gathering and work will also entail drawing the boundaries differently. Yet, just as in the case of cognitive disability, we can also accept that there are severe and central cases of loss of sight which we presume will be noteworthy in any human community and which will be universally problem engendering.

Cognitively disabled as a medical and scientific category

The physical basis of sight is the proper subject matter of scientific research and description. Sight is located in an identifiable organ, whose structure and functioning can be studied. Various impairments in sight can be related to precise features of this organ or to corresponding parts of the nervous system and brain. The manner in which diseases produce such impairments is known or, in principle, knowable. Ophthalmology and optometry can provide the agencies of the state with clear-cut definitions of blindness, so that they can, if they wish, have a precise medical basis for the decision as to who is to be registered blind and who not.[16] In this way precise sense can be given to 'blind person' if required. Medical science can measure sight.

How much of the above applies to science and cognitive disability? There are some close parallels. Science knows, for example, of many factors which produce varying degrees of cognitive disability. They include genetic anomalies, maternal and infant infections, different kinds of maternal and infant intoxication and disorders of metabolism and nutrition. More information on these fronts continues to emerge as research advances. But there are strong disanalogies between sight/blindness and intelligence/cognitive disability. Intelligence and cognitive skill are not known to have a physical organ or seat in the way sight is. Of course, it can be said that intelligence depends on the brain, but there has been little success in providing any precise physical correlate to intelligence either in a particular part of the brain or in identifiable, systemic features of the brain's functioning.[17] Such physical grounding faces problems of principle, since there are grave doubts (which will emerge below) as to whether there is a unified human capacity called 'intelligence'. If there is no such thing, then there is nothing to find a precise physical correlate to. There are forms of cognitive disability which appear to have no cause in organic brain damage. There is indeed the equivalent of optometry in psychology – psychometrics – which might claim to give a precise measurement of intelligence and its lack, but there turn out to be major problems with the scientific measure of intelligence. These points raise the doubt as to whether 'cognitive disability' can ever be translated from a social category into a scientific/medical one. While medicine and science may have much to say about specific forms of cognitive disability, there may be no conceptual room for a science of cognitive disability as such.

Cognitive disability (styled as 'mental handicap', '-deficiency', or '-retardation') has figured in twentieth-century science as a medical and diagnostic category. In the diagnostic handbook of the American Association on Mental Deficiency (AAMD), treated as definitive by many, 'mental retardation' is defined as 'significantly sub-average general intellectual functioning existing concurrently with deficits in adaptive behaviour and manifested during the developmental period'.[18] 'Developmental period' refers to the time from birth to 18 years and it figures in the definition in order to distinguish cognitive disability from mental illness and those impairments of mind evident in, for example, adult victims of strokes or dementia. The nub of the definition is in the two criteria of sub-average intellectual functioning and concurrent difficulties in social functioning. These conditions are treated as separately necessary and jointly sufficient (when combined with the condition of manifestation in the developmental phase). We have already prepared the ground for seeing why appropriate social functioning is included in defining the class: many individuals classified as disabled by intelligence tests alone are, or become, invisible to society and its agencies in adult life. They have sufficient cognitive abilities to adapt to, and function in, modern society without external support. To call them disabled would be odd. The presence of this necessary condition means that the AAMD's classification scheme cannot escape the shifting and relative character of social demarcations of the cognitively disabled noted in the previous section. The AAMD manual implicitly accepts this when it states that deficits in adaptive behaviour have to be judged against the background of what is 'expected' of the individual's 'age level and cultural group'.[19] It is an accepted fact that what it is to function successfully may vary with the patterns of life of different communities. The multiethnic character of North American society was no doubt before the mind of the diagnosticians. So we are still stuck with a category which has a significant penumbra. Membership of this penumbra is in turn influenced by factors relative to varying social circumstances.[20]

That IQ scores serve only as a necessary condition for the demarcation of the cognitively disabled shows of itself that psychological science can provide no precise demarcation of this class. There are yet further problems with reliance on IQ scores which cast doubt on their diagnostic usefulness in this area.

Note first that the use of IQ scores is meant to give precision to the condition that the cognitively disabled have 'significantly sub-average general intellectual functioning'. In the construction of IQ measurements, 100 is taken to be the average score of the general population. Fifteen points represent a standard deviation from this average. It is customary to take two standard deviations below the average as indicating significantly sub-average performance. Hence an IQ score of 70 is specified as the upper limit of disability. The AAMD's diagnostic criteria recognise that measuring IQ is not an exact science, so 70 is taken to indicate a broad band of about 66 to 74 and not a precise cut-off point.[21] More worrying than this imprecision is the fact that the IQ criterion once more introduces a marker for cognitive disability which is relational: it is IQ score relative to average performance for the general population (standardised for calendar age) that counts. It is plainly conceivable that someone's intelligence was significantly below the average of his/her peers and yet perfectly adequate for him/her to function as a planning, rational independent agent in society. All will depend on how high average intelligence is. This worry about the IQ criterion is not just theoretical. Evidence has been presented that average intelligence in societies such as the USA and Japan has risen over recent decades. That is to say, if judged by the norms applied to IQ sub-tests in the past, later populations would average at over 100 on their overall scores.[22] An average score of 100 on later norms represents an increase in intelligence, insofar as this is measured by IQ tests. People whose intellectual functioning would not have been at least two standard deviations below the average on the old norms would be if later norms are used to fix IQ scales. But their cognitive abilities would not have changed.

The problems with IQ measurement and cognitive disability mount once it is further realised that IQ is a highly selective and controversial measure of intelligence. Its selectivity and controversial status is a direct function of the history of IQ. The tale of IQ and its many deficiencies as a test of intelligence has been told over and over again and I do not wish to repeat the details here.[23] The case for the limited value of IQ as a measure of intelligence may be briefly summarised as follows.

The standard IQ tests and scales in use today (such as the Stanford-Binet Scale, the Wechsler Adult Intelligence Scale and the Wechsler Intelligence Scale for Children) all retain traces of their origins in the original intelligence tests devised by the French educational psychologist Alfred Binet at the beginning of the twentieth century. Binet created easily conducted tests to enable the French Ministry of Education to decide upon school and class placements for children. Because of these origins, IQ tests remain heavily biased to select skills valued in formal schooling in modern society. However, from the beginnings of their introduction, they were associated with a popular belief among educational psychologists that there is a unitary human power called 'intelligence' which lies behind the performance of human beings in all contexts requiring judgement, inferential skill, acuity in reasoning and so forth. But IQ tests have failed to serve as the measure of this postulated general power. From early on it was obvious that subjects perform differently in different IQ sub-tests, so that an overall IQ score must average out apparently separate skills. Critics argue that overall IQ score is not a good predictor of success or failure in intelligent activity outside formal schooling. It is not a reliable indicator of how well people will perform in varied employments or post-scholastic activity (though it should be noted that this claim is disputed).

There is a great deal of evidence to show that that which we call intelligence is context-dependent. People's ability to perform intellectually demanding tasks is heavily influenced by the context which surrounds them. For example, studies have shown that unschooled child street vendors in Brazil have mastered complex arithmetical skills. But they are unable to reproduce these skills in the artificial circumstances of an IQ test.[24] It makes all the difference that the mathematical puzzles they solve in real life are embedded in a context. They cannot abstract the skills involved from that context. It is, of course, a significant fact that formal schooling in the West teaches children intellectual skills in a context divorced from practical life. IQ tests also show this abstraction of skill from context. It is notable that many of our judgements of people's intelligence are context-rich. We judge people to be intelligent in performing music, or making conversation, or in doing logic, or in solving practical problems and so on. There could only be a scientifically measurable correlate of we what we call 'intelligence' if intelligence were truly a natural kind. If it were so, the varied, contextually-shaped forms of intelligence would be manifestations of an underlying, organically-based power. The presence or absence of that power would be displayed in the context-rich manifestations of intelligent thought, speech and activity. IQ would then function as the measure of this power. But the very fact of the contextual character of intelligence as we know it is a reason to expect that no such power is invisibly present in intelligence as we observe it. Nothing is more common than to find that a person who can manifest one form of context-rich intelligence cannot manifest another form.

In addition to the failure to provide (via IQ tests and scales) a measure for a uniform, context-invariant power called 'intelligence', psychologists have notably failed to provide a theoretical definition of intelligence which advances upon the non-technical notions of good sense, good memory, quickness in judgement and the like with which we are familiar in ordinary life. Still less have psychologists been able to point to a part or systemic property of the brain which might be the seat of a power of intelligence.

If the above case is sound, then there is no good reason to think we have a notion of intelligence which picks out a property whose presence, absence or degree we can measure in a scientific manner. Psychometrics is not the measurement arm of a genuine science of intelligence. It is not like optometry. Here is a verdict of two psychologists asked to contribute to a volume on mental deficiency as *defenders* of the usefulness of IQ testing in this field:

> We believe . . . that the most fundamental failings of such tests reside in their metric inadequacy and theoretical poverty. On these grounds alone, we suggest that psychologists abandon any inclinations they may have towards regarding IQ tests as instruments for measuring intelligence.[25]

If IQ is not an instrument for measuring intelligence, then it is not an instrument for measuring its lack. Adding it to a diagnostic definition of cognitive disability cannot add precision to the exercise of picking out a class of cognitively disabled people.

This critique of IQ does not entail that IQ has no value at all in studying and helping the cognitively disabled. The authors just quoted go on to list ways in which IQ can have diagnostic and predictive value in some contexts involving the cognitively disabled. IQ test batteries contain items which match closely to scholastic skills and they can thus be of use in deciding upon appropriate school placements. They typically contain sub-tests which enable a subject's mastery of vocabulary and grammar to be gauged and linguistic comprehension to be measured. They can thus give measurements of current linguistic functioning and of improvement or deterioration in linguistic functioning over time. They may provide predictions of future levels of linguistic performance. It is as an overall, and putatively scientific, measure of ability/disability that IQ fails. Over and over again we encounter the message that the final test of who is and who is not disabled is how people function in real life, in society: 'Recent work with handicapped persons suggests that formal measures of IQ, verbal and reasoning ability and social maturity are not clearly predictive of their ability to solve real problems'.[26]

My conclusion on IQ and cognitive disability is mixed: it provides no scientific measure of intelligence but it may be of assistance in diagnosis and prognosis. It should be noted that there is a much more radical case against the use of IQ in relation to the cognitively disabled. It is argued that IQ and psychometrics are inherently tied to an oppressive set of social practices whereby social norms favoured by dominant economic and racial groups are enforced upon others. This radical critique draws upon a number of points, including: the historical association between the intelligence testing movement and racial, eugenic theories of Social Darwinists, the alleged cultural bias in some standard test items and the fact that minority ethnic groups, such as Afro-Americans perform significantly worse on average in IQ tests.[27] Radical critics of the role of IQ in diagnosing cognitive disability, such as Jane Mercer, will link these factors by contending that IQ test batteries naturally produce lower scores for ethnic minorities because they are culturally loaded. They are designed to allow dominant groups in society to label others as 'retarded' and then to exclude them from normal schooling. IQ is a spurious, ideological justification of the practice of putting some people into disadvantaged social roles in order to preserve the interests of others.

The notion that classifications such as 'cognitively disabled', 'mentally retarded' are oppressive and ideological in function will be discussed at length in Chapter 5. Let us note some preliminary problems with the thesis. That some IQ sub-tests have a cultural load, if true, does not entail that all do. There are ways in which IQ tests can be helpful in diagnosis and prediction in facets of cognitive disability. There is, as we have argued above, a reality of human impairment and disability behind the various attempts to produce criteria to detect and measure disability. There are species-typical powers of cognition vital for human functioning. It can be evident from individuals' behaviour and development that they lack some or all of these powers to some degree or other. Many societies mark out people who have these disabilities. The view that being cognitively disabled is nothing but a social role is very hard to maintain consistently. Even radical critics of the IQ movement such as Jane Mercer have to accept that there are organically-based conditions such as Down's syndrome and that people with these conditions exhibit genuine symptoms of cognitive disability. It is, however, problematic to suggest that symptoms of disability are only real if we can find some organic cause of those symptoms. Presumably, in the vast majority of cases of organic, pathological conditions in the area, individuals were first noticed as having impairments of cognition of one sort or another. The discovery of organic damage underlying these symptoms came later. For a period, the outward disabilities would have been the only known factors identifying the condition. It is odd to suppose that they became real only on acquiring an organic explanation. Autism, which we shall discuss below, now exhibits this pattern: a distinctive array of cognitive defects has been noted but the search for an underlying organic pathology is still in its infancy.

Mercer contends that an inherent confusion arises in models of cognitive disability when IQ is introduced into the field. The confusion is between statistical and pathological models of disability. Disability as defined by IQ is a notion of the abnormal as judged by reference to the average performance in a given population. But cognitive disability defined in terms of some organically-grounded defect in cognitive powers is a quasi-medical notion with links to the idea of an organism whose functions have been interfered with.[28] Contrary to Mercer, there need be no confusion in understanding cognitive disability so long as an IQ score significantly below the average is not taken to be an absolutely sufficient condition in defining disability. The primary reality is the lack to some significant degree of species-typical powers necessary for functioning. IQ scores may be one helpful indicator of that lack even though they cannot be used as the means of defining it on their own. The search for organic defects underlying lack of species-typical powers of cognition can be seen as reflecting the important heuristic rule to seek organic causes of cognitive disabilities wherever possible. But we need not elevate the discovery of such causes into a necessary condition for the presence of the primary reality of cognitive disability. Thus use can be made of IQ scores along with the search for organic causes of cognitive impairments without the result that two different, exclusive definitions of 'cognitive disability' are forced on us. (The issue of the relation between sub-average intelligence and the existence of organic, diagnosable conditions will surface again in the next section of this chapter.)

For the above reasons, there is no need to choose between the rival views of IQ as the key arm of a genuine science of cognitive disability and of IQ as the key agent in an oppressive system of social control. IQ may be valuable in some respects, but be a limited, partial diagnostic tool in others. Some people may have indeed put IQ to ideological, oppressive use without the very notion being defined by that use.

We may sum up the case against there being a medico-scientific class of the cognitively disabled to replace the vague and shifting social-administrative one as follows. Even if intelligence and deficiencies therein were the way of demarcating the category, measuring intelligence cannot provide a scientific basis for the job. There is no science of intelligence. While there is a wide range of theories of intelligence in psychology, there is no agreement on which, if any, is correct and no prospect of establishing that agreement.[29] There are no proven ideas about the biological substratum of intelligence. There are no satisfactory measures of intelligence, indeed no agreement on whether there is a unitary trait of human beings called 'intelligence' capable of being measured by some yet to be discovered means.

Autism and intelligence

It is my belief that the existence and character of autism provides a further reason for objecting to the use of IQ in the demarcation of cognitive disability. Relying on some measure of IQ intelligence as either a necessary or a sufficient condition for the presence of cognitive disability will not encompass all the disabilities of autistic individuals and it will hide what makes autism truly disabling. There is indeed a real relationship between autism and whatever is measured by IQ. A clear majority (over three-quarters) of those diagnosed as autistic will have IQ scores below the magic 70. Some 60 per cent are likely to have scores below 50, thus making them severely retarded. Scores on IQ sub-tests have been shown to provide reliable indicators of aspects of the linguistic and cognitive skills of autistic children.[30] But despite autism and retardation as measured by IQ being related in these ways, autism is not the same as a lack of IQ measured intelligence. There is a significant if small class of autistic individuals who score above 70 and some, in particular those with Asperger's syndrome, with above average intelligence. Moreover, the impairments characteristic of autism are not found in the typical child or adult diagnosed as retarded by psychometric criteria. Autistic impairments are frequently accompanied by those associated with intellectual retardation but they are not the same as the impairments amounting to retardation. (This naturally invites the inference that whatever causes autism has a tendency, but no necessity, to cause retardation.)

Autism thus gives us a simple argument for the conclusions that cognitive disability does not consist in a significantly below average IQ intelligence and that low IQ is neither necessary nor sufficient for cognitive disability. The cognitive disabilities of autism are present in some people who have normal or above average IQ intelligence and they form a further level of disability in those with below average IQ intelligence.

The chief characteristic impairments of autism are threefold. First, there are impairments in social interaction, showing in difficulties with social relationships, in the understanding of others or in odd or naive social approaches. Second, there are related impairments in social communication, manifested in delayed acquisition of language and such things as difficulties in understanding the nature and meaning of communicative acts, both verbal and non-verbal. Third, there are impairments in the use of the imagination, showing in lack of creativity in play as a child and repetitive forms of behaviour throughout life. Further symptoms of autism present in many with the condition include the following: perceptual abnormalities, displayed in problems in focusing on, and discriminating between, sensory stimuli; ritualistic, obsessional and compulsive behaviours; and marked resistance to any kind of change in environment and routines.[31] As noted above, these symptoms are not simply a function of mental retardation. For example, the language deficits of the autistic are not the same as the deficits of those who are retarded. A Down's person may have acquired functional language late in development, compared with normal infants, just like one afflicted with autism. But the autistic person will in addition be noted for such things as: inability to take turns in conversation, literalness in the understanding of speech and monotonous descriptions of one subject regardless of the interlocutor's interest.

Autistic impairments are cognitively disabling over and above any lack of intelligence as measured by IQ. Autistic subjects have problems in understanding their world, not least because they have problems understanding and relating to people. The ability to adapt to a changing environment and to plan actions within it is impaired. Even autistic people with normal or above average intelligence measured by formal tests of abilities in reasoning, discrimination and calculating may thus require assistance from society. They come to notice as people who in one way or another have problems functioning as autonomous, planning and adaptive agents in the social world. The rigidity in their behaviours and the limitations in their imaginative powers make it difficult for them to formulate plans and execute them.

The deficiencies in pretence and imagination typical of the autistic entail difficulties in functioning as planning agents. Studies have shown that when autistic children are tested with puzzles (such as 'the tower of Hanoi') designed to bring out their ability to choose between one option and another in the light of their possible consequences, they are significantly poorer in execution than children matched for their mental age by means of IQ. Puzzles which ask them to choose between alternatives and in which, to make the choice, they need to imagine what would happen if they chose one alternative rather than another cause them problems. This is because they find it difficult to grasp a possibility which is removed from the actual state of affairs which confronts them. They find it difficult to envisage a non-existent hypothetical state of affairs and predict what would happen in that case.[32] This impairment must strike at the heart of anyone's ability to function as a practically rational agent. The characteristic resistance to change and addiction to routine may be a mechanism to defend against this significant deficiency in what is a key adaptive, cognitive skill.

Impairments in imagination affect autistics' ability to function as planning agents. In addition, the fact that autistic people have severe problems understanding others places severe limitations on their ability to understand and plan courses of conduct in a social world.

Studies have shown that a high proportion (some 75 per cent) of testable autistic children fail 'false belief tests' at a mental age when normal and Down's children pass. A false belief test typically takes the following form: the child has before it two boxes, two dolls and a sweet. The researcher ostentatiously places the sweet in box one in front of both dolls. Doll A is then taken away. Doll B naughtily moves the sweet to box two. Doll A is reintroduced and the child is asked where doll A will look for the sweet. Autistic children of high enough intelligence to be tested will show a marked tendency (as compared with matching mental age controls of normally able and Down's children) to say that doll A will look in box two, where the sweet actually is. The fact that doll A could only have the belief that the sweet is in box one does not register with the typical autistic child. This is indicative of a lack of, or delay in acquiring, the concept that the beliefs of others may be different from one's own and may be false.[33] Normal children will acquire this concept after their third birthday. The lack of a concept of false belief is not universal among autistic children. Between 20 and 25 per cent of autistic children with an IQ of 70 or above and a mental age of at least 3–4 years pass the false belief test. And many autistic children get over their blind spot about false beliefs as they get older. There is a graded impairment in autistic people's lack of understanding of others.[34] This means that even where the concept of false belief is acquired, autistic people have problems understanding and predicting the behaviour of other people, problems which are in addition to any degree of mental retardation they suffer. For example, it is well known that adults with Asperger's syndrome, who by definition have normal or high IQ intelligence, and who may well pass false belief tests, have great difficulties forming friendships with others and in understanding others' emotions.[35]

Various studies have shown that the impairment in understanding others goes deep into the earliest phases of an autistic child's development. Lack of shared attention behaviour in an infant is highly diagnostic of developing autism.[36] What is in question here is not the ability of an infant to get attention by gesture and voice to something it wants (attention behaviour which is instrumental), but rather gesture toward something so that the infant's reaction to it can be shared with the carer. Here the infant seems to seek shared attention for the sake of the emotion or feeling thus generated. The lack of this behaviour in autistic infants means that they are cut off from an important way of relating to, and learning from, others and may explain their later inability to appreciate others as having their own perspective upon a common world of objects and events. Observed lack of 'social pointing', of declarative attention behaviour, helps produce a cognitive outlook which cannot appreciate that one object can give rise to different reactions from different subjects, each with their unique perspectives on the world. This cuts autistic children off from an important source of learning, namely the reactions of others. It links to a characteristic later inability among those autistics who master language to appreciate speech as a means of exchanging information. The autistic speaker typically finds it hard to appreciate and partake in genuine conversation, the give and take of viewpoints. A sense of one's self as one among many selves is lacking or impaired. Hence, the naive and odd uses of language and the malformed ways of relating to others. Autistic individuals test poorly on scales of social and adaptive behaviour when matched against subjects with the same IQ mental age, supporting the claim that social criteria most robustly predict a diagnosis of autism.[37]

There is a variety of views as to the cause and underlying nature of autism. Debate on their merits is hampered over whether to classify autism as a discrete syndrome, albeit presenting in different ways in different sufferers, or as a spectrum of disorders, the instances of which are linked by family likeness. If the former model is adopted it is reasonable to seek a unitary cause of autism, or at least a final common pathway through which multiple causes trigger the syndrome. If the latter model is preferred, then there may be no single cause or single, final pathway.[38]

Within the variety of recent theories about the underlying nature of autism there is agreement on the failure of earlier attempts to explain autism as a result of poor or strange patterns of parenting. Hypotheses by psychoanalytic theorists such as Bettelheim to the effect that autism arises as a reaction to emotionally withdrawn or distant parents have proved to lack any empirical support. Autism afflicts children from all manner of parental backgrounds. Its precursors, such as lack of shared attention behaviour, are visible in very early infancy. It has been found that children brought up in institutions, where they lack the emotional richness of normal parenting, are no more likely to develop autism than children from the general population.[39] Current contenders amongst causal theories of autism thus turn their attention to pre-birth pathways which are more likely than not to be genetically influenced. Twin studies support this general contention.[40] Disagreement exists as to what kind of brain damage is the final causal pathway, if indeed there is one single one, for the production of autism. A number of theories opt for a defect in specific cognitive powers which then cascades down to produce the range of autistic symptoms. Thus it is contended that there is a specific module in the brain responsible for the ability to represent the mental states of others. This 'hardwiring' in the brain is damaged in the autistic. They cannot represent the mental states of others. They thus cannot understand others and their inability to 'mind-read' produces all manner of secondary effects.[41] A problem with this theory is that, as noted above, many autistic children and adults acquire the ability to represent others' states while continuing to manifest autistic symptoms.

If, on general philosophical grounds, one is convinced that the ability to mind-read depends not on having concepts for others' mental states but on the ability to simulate them in the imagination, then the way is open to explain both the mind-reading deficits of the autistic and many of their other disabilities through the hypothesis that the core ability to think imaginatively is impaired in autism.[42] As against this theory, one might be impressed by the fact that the autistic typically have difficulties not just in understanding others and in thinking imaginatively, but also in ordering information in a wide range of contexts.

Uta Frith has hypothesised that what is damaged in autism is some part(s) of the brain which gives us the ability to impose order on incoming information. Autistic people lack in some degree a central cohesive power which enables human beings to make coherent patterns out of disparate data, a power which depends in part on a further ability to detach cognition and attention from particular stimuli in order to see their place in a whole. The difficulties in understanding the actions and thoughts of others and in free, imaginative thought are consequences of this underlying impairment.[43]

The dominance of cognitive theories of the autistic deficit is balanced by those hypotheses which see an important affective and relational element in the aetiology of autism. Peter Hobson, supported by evidence about marked lack of attention-sharing behaviour in autistic infants, proposes that we should view autism as rooted in an inability to experience affectively co-ordinated interpersonal relations.[44] This entails an impairment in the ability to share social meaning. Patterns of social meaning in the form of shared concepts provide the means whereby we interpret the world. So the autistic's experience of the material and social world is disordered.

We cannot adjudicate on these different theories in this study. Their importance lies in the fact that they underline the manner in which the impairments of the autistic issue in major problems in understanding the world and people and in manifesting rational agency in the world. Thus autistic people may be said to be cognitively disabled. Autism meets a crucial element in the AAMD's criteria for cognitive disability in that it is a disorder of development, diagnosable in early childhood. And it meets the other non-psychometric criterion of the AAMD's definition of 'mental retardation': 'significant limitation in an individual's effectiveness in meeting the standards of maturation, learning, personal independence, and/or social responsibility that are expected of his or her age level and cultural group'. Yet we have seen that impairments in the autistic spectrum can be present where IQ intelligence is normal or above average and that these impairments supervene on top of those associated with lack of IQ intelligence. Hence, autism does indeed provide decisive evidence against using psychometric measures as necessary or sufficient conditions for the presence of cognitive disability.

Severe versus mild cognitive disability

If there is no science of cognitive disability, there is still a great deal that medicine and science can say about forms of impairment in cognition and intellect. Many such forms can be correlated with specific types of scientifically describable cause. As noted above, these causal factors include genetic anomalies, maternal and infant infections, different kinds of maternal and infant intoxication and disorders of metabolism and nutrition. Within these types of cause many sub-types have been identified and explored. So, much disability in cognition can be illuminated by science and medicine. Some authors think that the problems constructing a science of cognitive disability can be mitigated if we distinguish between, using their terminology now not mine, mild and severe forms of mental retardation (or -handicap or -deficiency). Severe retardation may also be styled 'clinical' and mild retardation 'socio-cultural' or 'cultural-familial'. It should be noted that this division of mentally retarded people ignores more precise classifications. The WHO *International Classification of Diseases* distinguishes between mild mental retardation (IQ 50–70), moderate (35–49), severe (20–34) and profound (under 20).[45]

The contrast between the severe and the mildly mentally retarded is held to be supported by reflection on two factors: the aetiology of retardation and the relation between the retarded population and the general population. As to aetiology, it is claimed that 'Nearly all severely retarded children have demonstrable organic brain disease',[46] whereas this cannot be said of the mildly mentally retarded population. Organic brain dysfunction is indicated either by knowledge of a specific biological cause of retardation, such as in fragile X syndrome or in the fact that indicators of brain damage like the presence of epilepsy are much more common in the severely retarded population. The labelling of mild retardation as 'socio-cultural' or 'cultural-familial' indicates the hypothesis that the aetiology of much retardation lies in social and family circumstances. Alongside the alleged contrast in aetiology, it is suggested that the severely mentally retarded form a definite subgroup within the general population. Separateness is indicated by the alleged fact that the size of the population of the severely mentally retarded will not fall with a general rise in IQ levels in the population as a whole (as measured on old norms). In contrast, there are signs that the numbers of mildly retarded individuals in contemporary Western societies are falling. For example, a decline in the numbers of mildly retarded persons in Sweden is recorded, as measured by psychometric tests standardised 40 years ago.[47] The prevalence of severe mental retardation is reported in the same study as being invariant with respect to social class, whereas prevalence rates for mild mental retardation are strongly linked to social class, suggesting perhaps that mild mental retardation is at least part-caused by familial factors affecting the quality of nurture or environment. The strongest way of drawing the distinction with respect to aetiology and relationship to the general population is offered by those theorists who adhere to a 'developmental' perspective on mild mental retardation. Their central hypothesis is that much (not all) mild mental retardation is a function of the normal distribution of intelligence within the human population, which distribution is in turn a function of the interaction between genetic variation in the human population and the diverse environments of individuals manifesting that genetic variation. The existence of mild mental retardation, together with the correlation of its prevalence with the general distribution of intelligence, is thus to be expected, as is the absence of known organic brain damage in the majority of the mildly retarded population. This hypothesis suggests that there are no specific differences between the majority of the mildly retarded and the general population over and above a lower rate of cognitive development in the former.[48]

Some of the points made in support of the distinction between severe and mild retardation seem telling to the layman, but it must be said that a sharp contrast between these two types of cognitive disability is not altogether safe. As to aetiology, it should be noted that the quotation from J. A. Corbett given above continues '. . . and this [the presence of demonstrable organic brain disease] is also true of a substantial minority of the mildly mentally retarded'. The unreliability of IQ measures has been remarked on in this context too. Evidence suggests that many individuals with IQ scores above 50 have multiple disabilities, in just the same way as individuals with scores of lower than 50, and may need special services, including medical ones, throughout their lives.[49] Their multiple disabilities are suggestive of an underlying pathology manifesting in varied ways. One of the reasons why the numbers of the mildly mentally retarded may be declining is that the organic causes of some of these forms of retardation are related to maternal health and diet and thus to the pre- and peri-natal health of the child. So their socio-cultural origin relates to the greater likelihood of specific forms of external damage to those who are poorer or less well educated about matters dietary and environmental. Ideas about the aetiology of cognitive disability are subject to swift change. As noted in the previous section, it is relatively recently that hypotheses about the organic cause of autism have gained ground against psychogenetic theories. New organic causes of disability are being documented all the time. The work noting the existence of fragile X syndrome dates from the late 1970s onwards and has provided a known cause for a substantial proportion of mental retardation which previously had no precise aetiology.[50]

It appears, then, that there is no hard and fast distinction between a class of mildly and a class of severely retarded individuals. There is a gradation, whereby the likelihood of linking disability to known organic damage or dysfunction increases as measured IQ falls below 50, as does the probability of individuals needing social and medical services. The difference between 49 and 50 on IQ scales no more marks a division in nature than that between 70 and 69. The class of the cognitively disabled remains one which society has to pick out by reference to a rough and ready idea of successful cognitive functioning and capacity for autonomous living, ideas which are both vague in themselves and sensitive to different social contexts and the expectations those contexts place upon individuals. Within this socially defined class, there are many individuals and many conditions about which medical science has much to say. Distinct syndromes, such as Down's, which include cognitive disability in their symptoms, can be identified. Conditions, such as meningomyelocoele, which bring increased risk of cognitive disability can be described. But in the absence of a scientific definition and measure of intelligence or cognitive ability, there is neither a science of cognitive ability nor a scientifically demarcated class of the cognitively disabled.

The prevalence of cognitive disability or mental retardation is inevitably a matter of much dispute and will be judged differently by those with opposing views on whether IQ is sufficient for demarcation and on whether some noted deficit in social functioning is also required. Different estimates are given in the various sources cited so far in this chapter. Richardson and Koller's estimates seem to fall in the middle of the range: 9.4/1000 for the mentally retarded in general (as measured by an IQ of below 70), 4/1000 for severe mental retardation (IQ of below 50).[51] It cannot be stressed too much that the population of the mentally retarded in general (around 1 in a hundred) is a highly heterogeneous one. Some will have no known associated organic disorder, others will. In the latter group people with Down's syndrome will be the largest sub-population but there are many other syndromes and disorders besides. And within the class, but extending beyond it, will be all those individuals with some form of autism. According to a recent estimate, the autistic amount to 28500 persons in the UK population of 60000000 on a narrow definition of autism (roughly 5 per 10000) and about 57000 on the broadest definition (roughly 10 per 10000).[52]

We have noted that the heterogeneity among the population of cognitively disabled people is ignored by philosophers who want to use the cognitively disabled in order to make a point about the alleged existence of human beings lacking full moral status. However, we must accept that within the class of the cognitively disabled, regardless of definition and measure, there are many individuals who provide grist to this philosophical mill. This is so not least because we have seen that the philosophers' favourite marks of personhood (self-consciousness, autonomy and rationality) are tied to the acquisition of language. Major deficits in language are a characteristic of those whose cognitive development is delayed and impaired. Here is one estimate:

> Communication deficiencies have long been recognised as among the most conspicuous and debilitating limitations in severe developmentally delayed and multiply handicapped children. Nearly all autistic children with an IQ below 50 fail to acquire speech and language . . . Likewise about 75 per cent of all retarded children with IQs below 50 show severe limitations in acquiring functional communication skills.[53]

So we can be in no doubt that there are human beings who depart from the norm of typical cognitive functioning to the extent that they become targets for a philosophically motivated expulsion from the class of persons. In the next chapter we shall be concerned to marshal arguments against taking normal cognitive functioning for the human being as a necessary condition for moral respect.

3
The Moral Status of the Cognitively Disabled

Questions of method

The challenge to the moral status of the cognitively disabled cannot be met without considering questions of method.

Questions of method arise in the first place because the philosophical doubts about whether the cognitively disabled are to be regarded as moral persons are not just of academic interest. These doubts raise fundamental issues about what kind of society we want to live in, about how much diversity we are prepared to tolerate in it and, ultimately, about which of its children we allow to survive beyond infancy. The philosophical arguments considered in Chapter 1 challenge our fundamental moral and political sensibilities. If we find that, upon reflection, we cannot bring ourselves to make the changes in sensibility demanded by the arguments, that would appear to be sufficient reason to reject them.

That last remark raises the question of the relation between the principles and arguments of philosophical moralists and what is styled 'our intuitions', that is our moral convictions prior to the application of philosophical arguments to moral dilemmas. No one engaged in these debates doubts that at least some of these pre-philosophical convictions have to stand as unshakeable checks upon the adequacy of ethical arguments. Glover, for example, quotes from shocking letters sent by I. G. Farben Chemicals to the authorities at Auschwitz expressing satisfaction with the last consignment of women for lethal experiments, letters which complain only that the price per head was too high. He comments to the effect that if his philosophical arguments 'made even a small contribution' to encouraging the attitudes towards people displayed in the letters, they would be unacceptable.[1] But let us suppose the letters quoted had read:

In contemplation of experiments with a new soporific drug, we would appreciate your procuring for us a number of severely retarded people. We consider the price of 200 marks a retarded too excessive. We propose to pay not more than 170 marks a head.

Should not this provoke equal disgust?

James Rachels is one philosophical moralist who has addressed the troublesome point that his conclusions appear not simply wrong but shameful. He tells us that the divergence between pre-philosophical and post-philosophical convictions is to be expected and accepted:

> The idea that our intuitions are not to be trusted is central to the argument of this book. It is not surprising that our intuitions favour the traditional view I have been criticising – after all, we have been raised and educated in a society formed by these views.[2]

Rachels is working with an implicit, rhetorical contrast between an extant set of moral convictions which is to a large degree made up of inherited prejudices and a new, critical morality which has passed through the mill of rigorous argument. He acknowledges that he, and any moralist, must rely on intuitions, but affirms that the trick is to use as few as possible: 'Every concession to intuition is just that – a concession'.[3] The clear alternative to intuition is the necessity of pursuing arguments wherever they lead, entailing that we heed plausible general principles (advanced by philosophers) over suspicious intuitions. Rationality and clarity lie with the principles, prejudice and the dead weight of tradition with the intuitions.

There is absolutely no need to accept this rhetorical structure as the framework for a debate about the moral status of the handicapped. In fact, the structure is itself the outcome of prejudice.

First, we must note the prejudicial distortion inherent in using the term 'intuitions' to denote what stands against the principles and arguments of the reforming philosopher. The analogy on which this terminology draws is with the practice of the theoretical grammarian constructing a set of general rules enshrining the difference between grammaticality and ungrammaticality in a language. The grammarian will work backward and forward from intuitions concerning the grammaticality of sentences to principles. Principles will have to conform to what native speakers take to be centrally grammatical and ungrammatical. But the grammarian's principles will not have to conform to intuitions about sentences which are borderline cases. Indeed the principles established by reference to the central cases will help sort out the members of this class.

The analogy between the grammarian and the moral philosopher quickly breaks down. What stands behind my conviction that killing a new-born baby is murder is not an intuition on a par with a raw feel that an odd-looking sentence is nonetheless grammatical. For if I gave up that conviction about killing the new-born, my view of myself and my world would change dramatically. If I became convinced that the likes of Glover and Singer are right – that there are no direct reasons why killing the new-born is wrong – then I would also have to accept that the babies I had helped to nurture had not really *demanded* love from me. Their value rather was conditional upon the fact that I and my wife *chose* to give them a future and were thereby potentially adding to the stock of worthwhile lives existing in the future. Such a change in conviction would entail a complete re-evaluation of an important part of my recent life. I would have changed thereby. Grammatical decisions, for all that many people can get steamed up about them, are matters of social convention in the last analysis. Moral perceptions are self-involving and self-constituting. It may, and indeed often does, take an arduous exercise in self-knowledge to decide whether I really think some practice is right or wrong. My stock of moral perceptions is thus never complete and available to me in order to test proposed general principles against it. Considerable intellectual skills may be involved in a grammarian's efforts to formulate the rules of a language. But the effort to determine what our moral perceptions are and to formulate such moral rules and principles as give best expression to their rationale is an achievement of wisdom and self-knowledge. (This is one reason why skill in the task is not a function of the philosophical training given in contemporary universities. It is, rather, a function of development and maturity as a person.)

The language of 'intuitions' is further suspect in implying that what exists in contrast to the general principles in such books as *The End of Life* are at best bare hunches and feelings, at worst prejudices resulting from religious and social indoctrination. But this range of alternatives is absurdly narrow. Our culture is full of reflective and probing explorations of moral sensibility, explorations existing outside of philosophical texts. Imaginative literature is one source of these explorations, and in our society it has played a notable part in inculcating attitudes toward the weak, the innocent and the outcast, attitudes which are directly relevant to the issues raised by contemporary philosophical moralists.[4] It is wrong in general to suppose that moral knowledge and insight only get into gear once we are in possession of stateable moral rules and principles and that without them we only have hunches.

On reflection, it becomes evident that the principles and abstract arguments of a Rachels or a Glover depend as much on so-called intuitions as the moralities they oppose. Rachels' decision to base an ethics of homicide on the principle that only those with a biographical life deserve protection, while those with merely a biological life do not, would be insupportable unless he had already assumed that his intuition that killing a healthy, normal human being was a central example of wrongful death, whereas killing a severely retarded person was a borderline case – something up for negotiation in the light of the newly-minted principles of a rational ethics. If he shared my view that killing a severely cognitively disabled individual in cold blood is as central an example of murder as you can get, then he would never have set off in the direction he did. His principles have no greater authority than the authority of the initial decision to divide the cases in that way.[5]

The clash between what the philosophers say about the negligible or non-existent moral status of the severely cognitively disabled and widespread pre-philosophical convictions is well brought out in Cora Diamond's request that we consider our reactions to the rape of a severely retarded woman incapable of consent.[6] The horror and enormity of this is *increased* by our sense of the mental weakness of the victim. As noted in Chapter 1, that such folk can be wronged, and are thus under the protection of justice, is fully reflected in the content of our legal traditions.

The protest I have mounted against the attack on our pre-philosophical conviction that the severely cognitively disabled are people claiming the protection of justice, are people who can be treated unjustly, as when they are murdered or raped, may seem like the worst possible defence of prejudice against reason's demands. Surely it must be possible to argue that many of society's most deeply held convictions don't stand up to rational scrutiny? Consider how white South Africans' views about themselves in relation to their black neighbours have been exposed. Many whites have had to undergo a reform of their moral and political sensibilities. But we need not oppose this line of argument. If moral philosophers could work an analogous transformation of our pre-philosophical convictions about the disabled, then well and good. If they could show that these convictions were based on confusion, expressed the merest prejudice, or were self-serving and self-deceiving, then we would have to embrace the change in moral sensibility involved. Honest challenges of this sort to our convictions must be met, though the challenges, if effective, will have to take the measure of the strength and centrality of any views they seek to overturn.

The objections to the rhetorical structure of intuitions versus principles are not meant to suggest that deeply felt and widely shared moral convictions cannot be shown to be wrong by arguments. The rejection of the rhetoric of intuitions and principles is rather meant to indicate that the philosopher's method of challenging those convictions is misconceived. The method is misconceived because: it too easily assumes that a stock of moral perceptions is available; it places too high a value on producing a coherent set of rules and principles to order those convictions; and it naively thinks that the overall goal can be achieved through the application of philosophical skills.

What the rest of this chapter will show is that the challenges to our conviction that the severely cognitively disabled are persons under the protection of justice and obligations of mutual aid are themselves confused. An early sign of that confusion is revealed in an obvious disanalogy between the exposé of white racism and supremacy in South Africa and the philosophical assault on the moral personality of infants and the disabled. The exposé of racism is a call to *extend* justice to oppressed human beings. The philosophical assault is a call to *withdraw* our moral concern from some human beings.

Speciesism and the category of the human

Any worthwhile defence of the moral status of infants and the cognitively disabled must resurrect 'human being' as a legitimate moral category and enable us to say that just in virtue of being human a fellow creature has claims upon us of a stringent kind.

An objection to this direct response to the philosophical problems outlined in Chapter 1 will come from those who think that indirect means of bringing the disabled under the protection of customary morality are available. Rawls, for example, appears to offer such an approach in *A Theory of Justice*. For Rawls the possession of a moral personality is a sufficient condition for someone to enjoy protection from the institutions and principles of justice. Moral personality in turn depends on the ability to have both a conception of the good (that is, a rational plan of life) and a sense of justice.[7] If moral personality is also a necessary condition for moral status, then Rawls is bound to conclude with fellow contractarians such as Gauthier that infants and the severely cognitively disabled are non-persons. However, he is able to resist this conclusion by contending in the first place that the ability to manifest moral personality should be understood as the possession of a potentiality which will be manifested in the normal course of development. Infants are thus under the protection of justice. Rawls further contends that 'The risk to just institutions would be too great'[8] if we withheld the application of principles of justice from any human being. What Rawls is alluding to is a form of rule utilitarian argument. Reflection on the effect of introducing a policy of withholding the protection of justice from that class of human beings deemed not to have moral personality suggests that the new practice would be difficult to limit and control. General respect for just institutions would be weakened. For example, the unscrupulous might use the exceptions then built into the principles of justice to harm others for their own profit under the cloak of a warranted waiver of moral requirements. Such worries could be reinforced by the difficulties of deciding who exactly passes and fails the test for possession of moral personality (more on this below). It is best then to act as if all members of the species share the fundamental equality Rawls' theory of moral personality requires.

It would be wrong to deny the force of the Rawlsian argument altogether. But it cannot provide the main response to the philosophical attack on the cognitively disabled, for it does not rebut that attack by finding something *in them* which is worthy of our deepest respect and which shows the philosophical dismissal of their claims upon us to be wrong. Rather, it appeals to the interests of those not under direct threat from the manoeuvres of moral philosophers: if the manoeuvres succeed, just institutions will be damaged and injustice to some with true moral personality is likely to result. To make this concern the centre of our response to the philosophical challenge is to come dangerously close to admitting that there is nothing in the disabled as such which rebuts this challenge.

There is nothing in the cognitively disabled which will suffice to establish their equal worth with typically functioning human beings other than their humanity. It is in the light of the humanity they share with us that we must say they are our moral equals. Given this point, we must confront the charge of speciesism aired in Chapter 1. This is the charge that anyone who makes mere membership of the human species decisive in giving a creature intrinsic, special moral worth commits a sin analogous to racism's assertion that being of a certain race is decisive for deserving respect.

The first response to the charge of speciesism is that, as presented by the likes of Glover and Singer, it rests upon a significant intellectual confusion. Their opponents need to claim that being a human being suffices to make something the possessor of intrinsic worth. Being human is a sufficient condition for every human being to deserve a special kind of respect. Glover, Singer and others respond by saying that to make species membership important in that way is to deny worth to other kinds of creature. The way in which the argument of those who use the label 'speciesism' works is as follows. First, they assume that the assertion that all human beings are due a special respect just in being human must be covertly comparative in its meaning. That is to say, it *must* mean 'only human beings (or: 'human beings above other kinds of creatures') are deserving of this kind of special respect'. Second, they then get from the assertion of the link between worth and humanity the consequence that other creatures can be killed and harmed just because they are not human. From that consequence, they finally bring out the moral equivalence between the stance that all human beings are worthy of respect just in being human and racism. They establish via these means that anyone who asserts that being human is sufficient for respect must be claiming that being human is sufficient *and necessary* for respect.

This line of argument is clearly illustrated in Kuhse and Singer's 'refutation' of the doctrine that human life is sacred. They note that the doctrine of the sanctity of human life has power to defeat their own views about what makes lives worth preserving and defending only if being human is defined in terms of species membership – not in terms of the possession of the typical qualities of adult members of the species. 'The crucial mistake' in the sanctity of life doctrine is then said to lie in the fact that it draws a moral distinction between membership of the human and other species. So it is, allegedly, tantamount to asserting that it is legitimate to kill a dolphin or a chimpanzee just because such a creature is not human. But that is the morally equivalent of the racist reasoning which says that it is legitimate to kill black people just because they are not white.[9]

The confusion in this line of argument boils down to the assumption that a claim for shared humanity as a sufficient condition for intrinsic worth must entail the claim that humanity is a necessary condition for such worth. However, the proposition 'If you are human, you have special worth' does not entail 'Only if you are human, do you have special worth'. Someone could only think that there was no fallacy in moving from 'humanity is a sufficient condition for moral status' to 'humanity is a necessary condition for moral status' if they thought there was no intellectual room to assert the intrinsic worth of all human beings while leaving open the question of the status of animals. But why should anyone think that? It seems entirely reasonable to suppose that someone might be absolutely committed to the truth that all our fellow human beings are worthy of the same fundamental respect, because they are our fellow human beings, but consider that the question of how we should regard animals is still open and should be explored on its merits. The confusions in the arguments of those who spread the charge of speciesism abroad stem from their initial assumption that a claim that all human beings, just in being human beings, are worthy of a special respect can only arise in a context in which the worth of different kinds of creatures is being compared and settled. The claim that all human individuals deserve moral respect must therefore foreclose all debates about whether being another kind of thing (such as a dolphin, chimpanzee or intelligent Martian) is also a sufficient condition for having this kind of intrinsic worth. Why on earth someone committed to a version of the view that the lives of all human beings are sacred just because they are human should thereby be committed to foreclosing the question of what other kinds of beings have intrinsic, special worth is beyond me. To slap the label 'speciesist' on the stance that being a human individual is a sufficient condition for a special worth is indeed to foreclose on the possibilities of argument and debate, and it is to do so by the somewhat childish means of giving a position one does not espouse a naughty name.

It is true that the stance on intrinsic worth and humanity I have outlined entails commitments to the effect that facts about species membership – or better, shared relationship among members of a kind – are of moral relevance in some cases. Some might think that this in itself opens the door to allowing other sorts of kind-membership to be important morally. So, the justification of racism and sexism becomes easier. But there is no reason to attribute such a vague, permissive intellectual principle to the defender of the moral saliency of humanity. The racist or sexist is still taking kind-membership to be a necessary condition for respect. Moreover, the very assertion that shared humanity is sufficient for respect amounts to the strongest possible rebuttal of racism and sexism. Assertion of the salience of shared humanity affirms commitment to the principle of the moral equality of all human beings provided for us by Simone Weil.

The linking of the defence of the centrality of the human in our response to infants and the disabled to racism and sexism appears even more strained when we consider that racism and sexism are in essence moral corruptions which consist in imposing a powerful group's perceptions on the powerless, thus ignoring or suppressing what those without power think about themselves. Racism ignores or sets aside the fact that the members of the persecuted group have a view of their own. It imposes one group's understanding upon another group. But we cannot impose our understanding upon animals, or compare our understanding of their lot with theirs. We can only ask how we should treat them and only our understanding of things, not theirs, can be consulted in answering that question.[10]

The above point does not establish that the customary practices toward animals of a non-vegan society are right, merely that they cannot be wrong in the same way in which sexism and racism are wrong. The profound disanalogies between what philosophers style speciesism and the evils of racism and sexism are pithily summarised in Bernard Williams' comment that speciesism is more properly called humanism.[11] We ought to be puzzled as to why anyone ever thought that we might improve the lot of animals by attacking humanism. However, it must be conceded that one particular argument in favour of better treatment of animals is unavailable if we accept that being human is a morally significant fact about a creature. Some writers advance an argument based on the premise that, for example, we quite rightly do not use infants and severely disabled people in harmful medical experiments. We should not subject them to this kind of harm because they are weak and vulnerable. But by the same token we should not use animals such as mice and rabbits in such experiments, for they are weak and vulnerable too.[12] The reclamation of the humanist perspective stops any apparent inconsistency in the refusal to let the moral saliency of the weakness of certain human beings translate into giving a like moral saliency to weakness in animals. There is no inconsistency in this refusal: since it is weakness in the human being that is before our attention, not weakness *per se* but weakness in the human being.

The baby or severely disabled person is protected from harmful experiments just because it is a human individual. Is the mouse or rat then subjected to these experiments just because it is not human? No: anyone who agrees with this discriminating policy will think that there are relevant considerations to be adduced about what it is to be a human being and what it is to be a rodent which permit the discrimination. For all that, in some individual cases the grounds for the discrimination may be brought out by calling attention to facts about the human baby or disabled person which are only made salient by specifying that it is related to us as a fellow human being. How this may be done will be explored in the later sections of this chapter.

What the opponents of speciesism illustrate is a commitment to the following theory about moral reasoning: only if we reason about the moral status of individuals (that is, about whether they are worthy of moral respect) in terms of their occurrent, monadic properties can we avoid intellectual and moral corruption. If we admit relational properties of individuals in thinking about their moral status, such as that of being in the same species as other creatures, into the basis of reasoning about which creatures are worthy of moral respect, fallacy and evil must result. There cannot be any properties of things relevant to establishing their moral status other than their monadic ones. Using the fact of humanity as a morally relevant property offends against this principle. It also offends against a further, associated principle evident from the summary of utilitarian reasoning offered in Chapter 1 above, namely that only properties of consciousness (such as the satisfaction of preferences) are relevant in well-ordered moral reasoning. No doubt arguments for these two principles can be given. If we are persuaded by those arguments, we will indeed regard appeals to mere humanity in the context of debates about moral status as mistaken. But the character of the mistake, if such it be, cannot be brought about by slapping a label on those who reject the principles which implies that they are guilty of fallacy and prejudice. That implies that those labelled 'speciesist' lack a moral position which is capable of articulation and defence. Their views will simply not stand up to scrutiny – like the racist's. So they do not need scrutinising. It is precisely this end-point of pure and mixed utilitarian reasoning in bioethics which seems to me to evince fallacy.

It must be stressed again that neither the specific points in the above paragraphs nor the general rejection of the usefulness of the notion of speciesism entails any conclusions about how we should treat animals. It may be that, for example, our treatment of rodents in scientific laboratories is wrong and can be shown to be so. What is blocked is an easy (a too easy) slide from how we reason about prejudice and oppression in the human case to how we should reason about our conduct towards animals. That leaves the debate about the proper treatment of animals to be conducted along separate lines.

Talk of speciesism cannot, then, block the thought that being human may properly be, in and of itself, a morally significant fact about the cognitively disabled. There may be a fundamental moral equality between us all, unaffected by the degree of our cognitive and social functioning. What trumps any natural inequalities between us may simply be the humanist perception that we are morally equal in being human.

Being human

If we could find that being a human being was a sufficient condition for having moral standing, then many advantages for ethical reflection would follow. We would be able to use 'human being' as a primary term of moral evaluation. We would, for example, no longer think in terms of valuing lives but valuing people, human beings. Philosophers who use the language of valuing lives lead us into sources of confusion. Potential confusion arises out of the need to find a criterion for when the kind of 'life' they find valuable is present. We have noted the agreement that rational, self-conscious, autonomous life is to be preferred. But these traits arise in people gradually and may be lost gradually, so that their presence and absence does not provide a decisive benchmark for how people should be treated. No one would say that the normal child is a fully rational, self-conscious, autonomous creature by its second birthday. But it has been persuasively argued that a child of this age manifests the prototypes of these traits. It will have intelligible speech. It will be aware of parental standards and whether or not it is acting in accordance with them. It will be able to use language to describe and draw attention to its own actions. In short, it has a primitive awareness that it is one being among others.[13] None of these abilities emerge all at once and all develop further thereafter.

We may claim in the light of the above facts that it is much easier to judge when something is a human being than it is to judge when it is a rational, self-conscious, autonomous creature (at least after its birth – problems abound in judging the moral status of the human conceptus, as the next chapter illustrates). We may also argue that taking human beings as the object of evaluation avoids the notable drift to 'occasionalism' which the language of valuing lives encourages. The philosophers whose views were documented in Chapter 1 assume that we cannot say being a human being is in itself something of decisive moral significance. They think we must ask of any human being 'Does s/he manifest a worthwhile life, the life of a person?' The upshot of this way of speaking is to make 'person' not the name of a substance but rather of a state that substances, creatures, may or may not manifest. Human beings cease to be valuable as such; they are rather (if they are lucky) the occasions for the manifestation of a state of being which is intrinsically valuable. Not all human beings are persons according to this way of thinking. Even a human being who is now a person was not a person some time in the past and will probably cease to be a person at some future time even while continuing to be a human being. It matters not, then, that the thing we call a person is an individual organism, which has the identity of such over time, from birth to death. This is shown in Kuhse and Singer's statement that

> when we kill a new-born infant there is no *person* whose life has begun. When I think of myself as the person I now am, I realise that I did not come into existence until some stage after my birth.[14]

The influence of utilitarianism runs strong in this implausible assertion. Value is to be located in states of consciousness. Flesh and blood people serve as the occasions for realising these units of value. But those flesh and blood people are not objects of value in themselves – hence, the real problems utilitarians face over distinguishing the morality of killing babies and the morality of deciding not to produce new ones. Kuhse and Singer cannot think of themselves as primarily human beings and yet affirm what they do about the nature of persons. The human being has a continuous history as an organism. Its identity is determined by its existence as an enduring biological entity. It does not come into existence and go out of existence as it acquires and loses capacities of mind.

If we resist this occasionalism and fasten upon the enduring human being as the object of value, then we avoid further problems. We do not need to wrestle with difficulties arising from adult, normal human beings who are temporarily comatose. In one obvious sense, to kill such a person cannot be to violate his or her autonomy since a comatose person is not now autonomous. Yet judged in another light, s/he has the present capacity to be rational and autonomous, since the basic organic foundations for those traits are but temporarily incapable of functioning. If we focus on the enduring human being we avoid the artificiality in saying that a new born infant is not a person, not yet intrinsically valuable, though it will become intrinsically valuable sometime in the future. We can only value persons by way of valuing human beings (or other substances) – since 'person' is not the name of a stage of a human being or of some state which human beings may occasion. Hence, in valuing the human being, we value it throughout its history.

In saying why human beings are intrinsically valuable, we could, for the sake of argument, accept the popular philosophical line that the measure of value is rational, self-conscious, autonomous life. This would cohere with a long tradition of defining 'person' as that which is rational. Jenny Teichman quotes Boethius' definition of 'person': 'The individual substance of a rational nature'.[15] The use of 'substance' in this definition makes clear that human beings cannot be the mere occasions for the manifestation of personhood. A person is a substance and has the identity over time of such. Something can only be a person by being one or other kind of substance. In the world which we know of, persons are human beings – biological substances of a certain kind. But there could be other substances which are persons. Angelic substances, the divine substance, articulate Martians, dolphins and chimpanzees would be possible examples. Accepting this way of thinking about personhood and the linked notions of intrinsic worth, we may still conclude that every human being is a person on the grounds that every human being shares in the nature of humanity and having that nature suffices for being a person. The nature of the substance human being is rational. This is shown in the fact that, overwhelmingly, the typical human being comes to exhibit rational life in the normal course of development, indeed its species-typical life *is* that of a creature with rational agency and consciousness. In some human beings this nature is impaired but these human beings are creatures of a rational kind nonetheless, just as they would be if they had an unimpaired nature but never displayed a rational life because they were deprived of human nurture.[16]

An immediate advantage of the above reflections is that they enable us finally to bury the charge of unwarranted prejudice in favour of our own kind contained in the label 'speciesism'. Basing the intrinsic worth of all human beings on the fact that they all, *qua* human, share in rational nature entails no devaluation of other kinds of creatures. First, we may be persuaded that other things than being a person in Boethius' sense could be grounds of intrinsic worth. Debate on that score remains open. Second, the Boethian principle 'Whatever is a substance with a rational nature is of special, instrinsic worth' can be universalised with perfect consistency. If propagandists for dolphins and chimpanzees convince us that, in the normal, typical case, these creatures display rational life, then they too will count as persons and enjoy intrinsic worth. If it is a fact that only human beings are persons, it is an empirical one and thus not to be defended by moral stipulation. Consistently universalising the Boethian principle does entail that if we deem dolphins to have a rational nature, then baby dolphins, senile demented dolphins and cognitively disabled dolphins are persons as well and are to be treated as such – a conclusion which champions of the dolphin will surely welcome. No creature, then, need be denied moral status by the Boethian principle.

One important line of attack against the Boethian principle must be noted. The argument fostered by the principle is that, since all human beings are members of the same species, they all share the same nature and thus possess a natural equality which is the foundation of a shared intrinsic worth. It may be objected that this argument presupposes the implausible belief that there are essences and that possession of an essence unites those things we classify as members of a common bio-logical species. Yet biology has long since given up belief in essences. Species are no more than kinds created by the separation of breeding populations. Species are well-marked varieties apparently separate from other kinds only because the intermediate varieties which connect them to all other kinds have died out. All species have a history; all evolved out of earlier species; all are related to other species. These facts hold for *homo sapiens* as for any other species. Once we see human kind in an evolutionary setting then belief in the uniqueness of this kind is untenable.[17]

In reply, defenders of the Boethian principle should deny that they are at all committed to thinking that there are essences, in any sense of 'essence' which is metaphysically loaded. The nature which unites members of *homo sapiens* can be admitted to have a history. It can be accepted that this history is tied in with the history of animals such as chimpanzees and gorillas and that in consequence there is much in our genetic endowment which links us to other kinds of things. It can be accepted that if all the ancestor species to *homo sapiens* were still extant, then there would be a visible chain of kinds linking us to non-human forms of life. But it is nonetheless the case that our species evolved into a separate kind through evolutionary history. The species has developed characteristic properties so as to give us a sense of the typical traits and functions of the human being. To say that the human being has the nature of a rational kind is not to point to a mysterious metaphysical essence human beings possess, but rather to admitted, empirically discovered facts about our species – facts such as our learn-ing abilities, our capacity for complex forms of social existence and sym-bolic communication.[18] The Boethian principle need not depend on the argument that this nature is *separate*, that it is absolutely unlike the nature of any other kind. If the case that some mount for the higher apes as symbol-using, autonomous creatures be sound, so be it.[19] The Boethian principle should be universalised consistently, as noted above. More generally, the embodied character of personal existence in the human being should make us take very seriously the evolutionary affinity between ourselves and the higher apes in considering how we treat the latter.

The defence mounted against the charge of essentialism will be deemed inadequate by many who are informed by ecological consciousness. They will contend that, once we realise the inter-relatedness of living things to each other and to their environments, we will see that species distinctions are unimportant: there is no distinct 'us' that is *homo sapiens*. Stephen Clark summarises this thought as claiming that all material bodies and kinds have fuzzy edges. We should not assume that our language 'cuts the world at its joints' and that there are thus real individuals and kinds corresponding to our terms of classification. Instead, reflection shows that any individual or kind can be thought of as embedded in another, wider whole. Any living thing functions only as part of a larger segment, which in turn is part of larger and so on, until we see that the only proper object of respect is the terrestrial (cosmic?) ecosystem as a whole.[20]

The ecological case against counting human beings as constituting a discriminable rational kind can be read in two ways. It could be read as saying that the class of the human is an arbitrary one, or it could mean merely that for *some purposes* it is proper not to consider it separately, but as part of a larger system. We can recognise that our language may not 'cut the world at its joints' if this means merely that there are many types, wholes, in nature and which ones we recognise is partly down to us. It is a different, much more implausible claim, that there are no types in nature and all classification is arbitrary. It is this latter claim which is needed to defeat the notion that there is a rational kind called 'human being'. That the divisions we mark by 'human being' and *homo sapiens* are not arbitrary can be seen by reflection on the following facts. First a minor point: 'human being' provides us with a counting principle and a principle of identity over time. The question 'How many human beings are there in the room?' can be given a non-arbitrary answer, in the way that 'How many red things are there here?' cannot. For where do we say one red thing ends and another starts? By the same token, 'ecosystem' provides no counting principle but is dependent on attaching itself to a material substance term (as: '. . . of the earth'). Equally, use of 'human being' can provide us with a means of telling when a human being now is the same as one earlier. This is not to say that there can be no borderline cases in counting or re-identifying. But cases like those of Siamese twins really do prove the rule. A more substantive point: if human beings form a genuine kind, then we should expect that the study of some of them tells us lots of things about all of them. This is indeed so. Medical students see only a few examples of human anatomy, physiology and histology but become knowledgeable about the physical make-up of all of us – of the human being. Similarly we should expect, and indeed do find, that more and more qualities can be discovered about the human being. By contrast, there is little over and above being red which unites red things. The nature of human beings is thus a fit subject for scientific theorising and research.

It looks as though the term 'human being' picks out a genuine kind, one that is in the world and discovered rather than invented by us. The kind exists independently of our interests. The ecologist is right in suggesting that which kinds we choose to pick out may be relative to our purposes. Further, s/he will be correct in affirm-ing that for certain important purposes, scientific and ethical, it will be proper not to concentrate on kinds of organism but on func-tioning ecosystems and their properties. It may indeed be harmful when focusing on these purposes not to think in terms of larger wholes. There is absolutely no need for humanism and ecology to fight a battle over so-called essentialism, so long as each recognises that we can approach the world with different purposes on different occasions.

The important sense in which human beings share a common nature can be brought out by considering our perception of the cognitively disabled. Those classed as disabled are atypical. But they are not just different. Their difference rests on an impairment in an organ or in a functional sub-system of the human being. They thereby come to lack an ability typical of the human. Our capacity to think in these terms confirms our sense that there is a nature which human beings share, a nature which in turn adapts human beings to the per-formance of tasks in their environment. Two facets of the relationship between individual differences and our common human nature emerge. One is that there are limits to how far differences from typical structure can go in certain directions before they lead to loss or impairment of function. A second is that there are limits to how far atypical func-tioning can go before the individual who is different becomes mala-dapted by virtue of atypical functioning. For example, chromosomal abnormalities such as Down's and fragile X syndromes do not simply mark differences between a minority of human beings and the majority. Loss of some degree of cognitive functioning follows and that loss has implications for successful functioning in the complex social existence to which the species is adapted and which has enabled it to flourish.

These comments reflect the argument of Chapter 2 to the effect that there is an economy in human nature which shows apparent designedness toward the achievement of ends, an apparent designedness which is in turn the product of adaptive pressures upon the evolution of the species. They also connect with the argument that severe cognitive disability – such as might seriously impair rational and autonomous functioning – is not likely to reflect a natural variation in human intelligence, but should rather be expected to arise out of organic damage to the brain, however caused. If we consider the case of a creature such as a dog which is not a rational, language using animal by kind, then it makes no sense to say that it suffers impairment of function or has a disability because it cannot talk or reason. Its condition is not to be explained through diagnosis of how its canine nature is disordered through disease, malnutrition or congenital abnormality.

There is more to be said in defence of the notion that the cognitively disabled can be said to share a common nature, albeit one that is damaged and impaired. Most of us would find it natural to say that one who was severely cognitively disabled was not merely disabled, maladapted but also afflicted (in contrast to the viewpoint of David Pailin explored in the previous chapter). Yet it would make no sense to say of a dog, which can do the things dogs typically do, that it was afflicted because it cannot do the things a human typically does. Most of us would take it that severe cognitive disability should be prevented in future generations if possible and that those who suffer from it deserve remedial help. Again, none of this makes sense when applied to the dog's lack of rational powers. These thoughts fit in with the picture of something which has a nature damaged and hindered from flourishing. Such thoughts do not entail devaluing the person who is so afflicted. On the contrary, the structure of, and background to, the thought 'Here is one damaged and afflicted' take us in the opposite direction. The structure and background to our thought involve us in thinking of this human being as one with us, not as a different creature. As one of our kind, s/he deserves the respect due to beings of our kind and, despite the differences between us and him or her, we share a natural equality, possession of humanity, which is the basis of a moral equality. These equalities demand in turn that we aid this impaired member of our kind.

Thoughts about affliction take us beyond ideas of maladaptiveness. Consider the possibility that one who is cognitively disabled nonetheless adapts to the environment but by dint of functioning as an animal not a human being. Such an example is furnished by the case of the Wild Boy of Aveyron described by Uta Frith.[21] The Wild Boy was discovered by a French physician, E. M. Itard, in the last years of the eighteenth century. He had been living wild in the woods for what appeared to be many years. Frith argues that the child's symptoms point to autism, which in turn might suggest he was cast out by his parents, for after being under Itard's care for years he did not acquire language and remained socially impaired. I suggest that, even if we imagine the Wild Boy staying in the woods for the rest of his life and surviving successfully, we would regard him as afflicted. Though indeed adapted to an environment and surviving in it, he was not living as a creature of his kind ought to be. He was impaired and disabled. He was properly an object of the doctor's concern and aid and it was a good thing that he was helped to acquire some of the cognitive functions of his kind and enjoy some measure of a human, social existence.

I offer these thoughts about affliction as justification for the abhorrence which any right-minded person will have contemplating the suggestion (whether serious or not) from Frey and Singer that someone who is severely cognitively disabled might be used in research in the way we might use a rodent. For one who is so profoundly disabled as to have no language and little sense of self, or of past and future, is already one who suffers injury and harm. That should make unthinkable the option of hurting or killing them for others' benefit, for that would be to further injure and harm them. Now regardless of whether we think rats and mice should be used as experimental subjects in laboratories, they are not suffering an affliction in being so used which adds to their affliction in not being self-conscious, rational beings. That they are not self-conscious and rational is not a mark of affliction.

I submit that the arguments offered so far in this chapter give content and grounding to two vital parts of a humanist outlook. First, such an outlook contains a belief that there is a natural equality among all human beings consisting in nothing more, and nothing less, than their shared membership of the human race. Second, it asserts a moral equality amongst all of us based upon that natural equality.

Our moral equality consists in all of us being due the protection of the fundamental duties of justice and mutual aid. This equality obtains amongst us all, even though some few of us are never able to realise what these duties are and are thus not moral personalities in Rawls' sense.

Human being and rational being

A recurrent theme of this chapter has been the extent to which the philosophical attack on the moral status of the cognitively disabled entails a departure from customary moral insight and vocabulary. In response to this unwelcome thrust of contemporary bioethics, I have tried to argue for the legitimate status of the concept of human being as the foundation of our reasoning about how we should treat other people. However, the defence of the centrality of the concept of human being offered in the previous section is open to the objection that it gives too much to those who think that only philosophical theorising can put our moral judgements on a firm foundation. The argument which relies on the Boethian definition of 'person' may still be said to give the concept of human being a secondary and dependent role in our moral thought.

The argument advanced so far leaves the concept of humanity dependent upon the concept of rational being. The object of moral worth and respect is primarily rational being. Human being is valuable because it is rational being; for example, the wrongness of killing a human being is derivative from the wrongness of destroying a being who has a rational nature. Thus the plea 'they are human beings' is not allowed to stand of itself as a sufficient reason to rebut any lethal intent to the disabled. Something allegedly more fundamental must be cited and that thing is revealed by philosophical reflection, which is thereby accorded a status superior to thinking conducted in terms of our everyday moral concepts. Metaphysical insight into the nature of personhood must undergird moral insight.

An argument for rejecting the ability of philosophy to provide a more certain foundation for ordinary moral thought is provided by Anne Maclean. She examines the attempts of one notable bioethicist, John Harris, to replace our normal conception of the worth of human beings with the notion of beings whose lives are valuable. Valuable life, argues Harris, is life sustained by the reflective desire to go on living. Other things being equal, we may licitly kill both those beings without the capacity for having this desire and those beings who have a reflective desire for death. Such an account transforms our ordinary notion of murder and indeed jettisons many aspects of customary morality. It has the familiar consequence of leaving many types of human being unprotected by rules forbidding homicide.[22] Maclean's objection to Harris can be simply put as follows.[23] By the 'value of life' Harris does not mean to refer to anything as mundane as the value of life for the person concerned. We may recognise that someone's despair or depression is such that they no longer attach importance to continued existence. They may cease to find anything in life valuable. Harris wishes to make an inference from such facts to the philosophical conclusion that such a life has no value. The philosophical conclusion must say more than that the owner of the life no longer finds it worth living. Harris wants to infer that a life lacks value from the premise that it lacks value for the individual concerned. The conclusion does not merely repeat the premise; it draws a substantive consequence from it. Maclean says that Harris is employing such words as 'This life has value' in a metaphysical sense. That is, from the standpoint of insight into what is valuable in the universe, as it were, the philosopher discerns what is ultimately of value and uses this insight to reformulate morality. What is deemed valuable in the matter of life from this metaphysical standpoint is life supported by a reflective desire to go on living. But, argues Maclean, there is no reason to believe either that we can support conclusions about value from this metaphysical standpoint or that talk coming as if from such a standpoint has any clear sense.

Harris does of course argue for his conclusions about the value of life. But Maclean makes a point about these arguments similar to that made in this chapter about Rachels' arguments on the low value of mere biological life. The arguments offered depend essentially on moral verdicts on particular cases. They reason back from putatively sound judgements about the licit killing of classes of human being to a moral principle which will rationalise those judgements. Hence, the judgements about the value of life of the bioethicist can be given a sense after all. They are not made from some metaphysical standpoint 'at the centre of the universe' to which philosophy gives access. They are moral judgements on a par with ordinary moral judgements. The conclusion that life is valuable only if sustained by a reflective desire to go on living is the moral judgement that there is, at least *prima facie*, nothing wrong in killing people who are infants, permanently comatose, demented – or severely cognitively disabled.

What the philosopher has not done is provide a metaphysical foundation for a new, reformed morality. There is no privileged philosophical access to value which will serve to justify or refute fundamental moral claims. The pretence of so much philosophically backed bioethics to use philosophical theory to step outside ordinary moral judgement and discern what might be of value to some Ideal Observer occupying a view from nowhere *is* a pretence. It is, ultimately, the pretence that philosophy has access to transcendent modes of reason which operate independently of the modes of reason immanent in the moral life of human beings. There are modes of reasoning immanent in ethics. The philosopher might have specific insights into how these operate (but so might others, such as the novelist). What the philosopher must abandon is the false position that there is a rational answer to a question such as 'How should we treat the disabled?' to which philosophy gives special access independent of ordinary moral judgement.[24]

The error involved in seeking a philosophical-cum-metaphysical grounding of ordinary moral convictions is linked to the idea that we can, via philosophy, abandon a human point of view on the world and what is of value in it. No one will deny that we can reason about how we are to treat each other and the rest of the planet. But we cannot reason about those things other than by using insights and forms of argument immanent in human reasoning about value. Arguments to the effect that much of our past thinking about how we treat human beings, animals or the ecosystem has been misguided are possible. But they can only work in the standard way moral arguments do work. They must move from one moral judgement deemed fixed or central in the context to other moral judgements by analogy and difference. This does not put a block on moral reform. Indeed, it may be the case that the reform of our moral judgements advocated by contemporary philosophers could be presented as standard attempts to get us from one moral judgement to another. It may be argued that, despite the apparent violence they do ordinary perceptions about the value of infants and the like, the pure and mixed forms of utilitarianism do provide a cogent way of linking some moral judgements to others by likeness and difference. The authority of the principles advocated by proponents of these forms of reasoning would then depend upon the forms of understanding and judgement immanent in customary morality. It appears, however, that the arguments of moral theorists too often rest upon the pretence that we can rise above these immanent methods of conveying insight and gain agreement by means of a philosophical theory of the valuable based on transcendent reason. This pretence is false for the reasons given above.

Such pretension is apparent in the argument of the previous section to the effect that the reason why human beings are to be valued as persons is because they share in rational nature. This implies that the value of persons is derived from the value of rational nature. It implies that if someone can see no moral force in the fact that the other, whose existence they wish to write off as of no value, is a human being can have their moral sense rebuilt by citing the morally more fundamental fact that the other is a being with a rational nature. To think that support for our recognition of the other human being might be given in this way is to embrace a number of unlikely suppositions. It is implausible to suppose that the principle 'Beings with a rational nature have intrinsic worth' is more certain than a corresponding principle about human beings. If anyone genuinely thinks that 'Killing human beings is wrong' is either unclear or uncertain, they are hardly more likely to find the principle about rational nature clearer or more cogent. If I am recommended to value, in my actions and attitudes, beings of a rational nature, the most plausible justification for that recommendation would be that the recommendation reflected what we know to be morally demanded of us by our fellow human beings.[25] The clearest practical interpretation of the principle would be given by advice to be wary of committing or encouraging the wrongs to others picked out by our customary moral vocabulary, wrongs such as cheating, stealing, lying, neglect and so forth.

A further difficulty with the Boethian principle as a support for a foundational respect for humanity is that it restricts the sources of that respect, and for that reason does not ground it well. The Boethian principle narrows the grounds of worth to common possession of a species-nature which has a typical expression in rational life. But our concept of a human being is richer than that and other facets of it justly awaken conscience to acts which cause harm or show disrespect to others. In the first place, there is much more we share with other human beings than a species-nature. It may be worthwhile to inform unthinking writers in bioethics that we are all related to others as common members of a species. That may remind them, as we did earlier in this chapter, that the disabled are not merely different in certain respects from the typical human being but also afflicted. But that specific reminder about difference leading to affliction will be made more forcefully by seeing the disabled as specifically 'fellow human beings', and yet other reminders of disabled people's claims upon us will be brought home by that perception of them as fellow human beings.

Seeing the cognitively disabled as fellow human beings will remind us, for example, that like the rest of us they were born of human parents. And that fact will in turn bring to our attention that, as human babies rather than cattle on the farm, they were given names not numbers.[26] Their having a name is bound up with the fact that a Down's baby or an autistic three year old is still someone. They are still members of a human community. The humanity they share with us reminds us that Rachels' claim, noted above, that there is no moral issue in killing the severely retarded is tantamount to summarily expelling them from the human community. And it bids us demand of him, and people who think like him, the most stringent justification for such an expulsion.

The above considerations take us away from construing the fundamentals of our respect for the cognitively disabled in terms of their possession of a feature (such as, rational nature) and the value of that feature. It focuses attention instead on their being the fit objects of certain attitudes, where the fitness of those attitudes is bound up with the relations they stand in to others. So relationship rather than property possession serves as the foundation of respect.[27]

The point about relation can be brought home by recalling the account of Vicky from Pat Henton's 'Caring' first introduced in Chapter 2. Vicky's profound handicaps entail the most dedicated, unremitting care from Pat and her husband. Such care is the work of love. It is not done with an end in view, as a shepherd's care of an orphan lamb may be. It manifests a love which is purposeless, in the sense that the life of care flowing from it has its end within itself. The love and care is demanded by its object and the sense that it is demanded is no doubt one of the things that sustains Pat in her care. The care is not created by the adoption of an attitude towards the one cared for. That possibility would be exemplified in the typical case of the animal taken into a human home as a pet. The care and love lavished on a pet by a good owner is a consequence of the decision to make the animal into a pet. Outside of that relationship – adopted, chosen, by the human being – the care would be inappropriate. (No doubt some vegans and vegetarians would dissent from that last point.) But the love given to Vicky becomes immediately intelligible to us in the recognition that Vicky is a fellow human being, someone with a name, someone else's daughter. The unremitting character of the care she demands would strike most of us as bizarre if lavished on an animal. By the same token, if Vicky pre-deceases her parents, we will find it natural if they arrange a funeral for her. It would be unfitting from a moral point of view if they did not. It is not unfitting to dispose of a dead pet without a funeral.

The case that certain moral demands are rendered intelligible by the perception that another is a fellow human being has been made by drawing a contrast with the perception of another creature as an animal or pet. It might thus be thought that it breaches the claim at the start of this chapter to the effect the moral claims of human beings can be established without making comparative judgements about animals. However, the employment of a customary contrast in attitudes to the animal and the human is not necessary to make the point, albeit that it helps. We can imagine, and indeed find, religious conceptions (among others) which bring with them a sense of animals as 'fellow creatures' (all creatures enjoying a relation to God), perceptions which generate, for those whose thinking is dominated by such conceptions, a love for animals comparable to the love one human being can give to another. To such a person the perception of an animal as a fellow creature will suffice to create an identification with the lot of an animal comparable with the customary ability to identify with the lot of a fellow human being.

Handicapped children like Vicky can be rejected by their parents. Parents can be too upset or shocked to heed the claims of their child and its humanity. We may condemn this in the particular case. We may not, thinking only too clearly of what we might do if our love were tested so. The important thing in this context is to realise that the very vocabulary we use to describe such cases ('rejection', 'love being put to the test' and so on) is indicative of the fact that there is something special about the handicapped infant arising from its being a human baby.[28] The appropriateness of the vocabulary and its associated attitudes is of course totally ignored in the radical reconstructions of ethics from practitioners of bioethics. But this vocabulary is not given a foundation or grounding by talk of the baby sharing in rational nature. There are moral possibilities in our relations with human beings which can only be brought to mind by keeping the category of fellow human being fundamental in our thinking.

Practitioners of bioethics wish to displace the category of human being from the centre of our reflection about how we should treat others. It may seem as if they have reason on their side. It appears self-evident that we are constrained by the following argument. If I judge that all human beings have worth, there must be some property they all share which is the basis of that worth. Things not having worth will lack this property. So the judgement 'Human beings have worth' depends on the logically and ethically prior judgement that all beings with this specified property have worth. If your judgement about human beings is *grounded*, based on something answerable to *reason*, then the category of human being cannot be foundational in that judgement.

This argument fits in with a certain picture of the nature of moral evaluation. According to the picture, judging the moral value of acts or entities is a matter of first noting that they are similar in their possession of non-moral qualities and then deciding that things with those qualities are good or bad. Hence, a moral concept is exhaustively analysable into a descriptive classification plus an element of positive or negative evaluation. Thus if the concept of human being is used as a vehicle of moral evaluation, it can only be that a positive evaluation has been added to its descriptive meaning, 'member of the species *homo sapiens*'. The reforming moral philosopher will then claim, for all the reasons we have noted above, that it is arbitrary or discriminatory to attach a strong positive moral evaluation to this descriptive feature. Likewise, if moral condemnation is built into the concept of murder, it can only be because a type of action which can be naturally defined (as: killing beings of such-and-such type, in such-and-such circumstances) has been declared to be wrong.

Both the argument and the background picture against taking the concept of human being to be morally foundational are unsound. The abstract principle 'If we judge cases to be morally alike they must share some relevant similarities' is unobjectionable. But that principle does not entail that relevant similarities are discoverable without the guidance of the rationale contained within the relevant moral concept. The concept of murder is not simply the concept of a kind of act defined in natural terms which I and others then condemn. It signifies a moral category. Murders are not simply homicides which are deemed wrong. They are homicides for which none of the standard justifications of homicide apply.[29] The concept of murder contains a rationale which guides thought, a principle of likeness and difference which is an aid to discrimination. The rationale and discrimination in it would be lost if we attempted to cash it in wholly natural terms. It is in the light of its rationale that we can see the salience of a range of non-moral facts about actions. It is in this way that we could argue that the concept cannot be translated into a fusion of natural categories plus an element of evaluation.[30]

The philosophical attack on the foundational status of the concept of human being is based on an absolute refusal to accept that the concept can be anything other than a purely natural one ('member of a certain species') to which an element of evaluation has been attached in the past but which may be detached in the future. But it is open to us to contend that the notion of human being, with its resonance of 'fellow human being', is the means of moral discernment. It is the vehicle for moral discernment. In it and through it we make salient a wide range of facts about how we are related to each other as members of a community, such as the fact that we treat human beings as individuals by virtue of giving them names. The concept of human being introduces a way of seeing others which then makes a range of attitudes and responses appropriate. 'Human being' means more than 'member of a certain species'. If I say of an acquaintance 'He does not see his colleagues as human beings', I am not attributing a confusion about species to this individual, but commenting on the way he cannot confront others as individuals in their own right. One of the things Singer, Glover, Frey, Rachels *et al.* wish to do in asking us to displace the concept of human being from the centre of our moral thinking is to forget that it is natural for us to view human beings in distinctive ways and that such modes of vision are connected with a range of equally distinctive attitudes. To deprive us of the concept of human being in reflecting on the cognitively disabled is to banish the memory of the ways we can view and respond to them as fellow human beings.

The philosopher's view of the nature of moral concepts (and of the concept of human being) makes external criticism of our modes of moral judgement easy. The rationale of those modes of judgement is deemed to be cashable in terms which are independent of the concepts shaping them and embedded in them. There is no vision, insight in these practices (as opposed to prejudices) which cannot be articulated in concepts independent of them and based on non-moral modes of discernment. A transcendent reason forged independently of the insight within our moral categories can then decide whether these our customary judgements are correct or not.

The picture of moral concepts I have defended makes external criticism of our moral practices correspondingly more difficult. For the question of whether those practices embody insight or illusion cannot be settled by laying out their rationale in independent terms. The matter cannot be judged by a transcendent, decontextualised reason. Rather reason operates in ethics properly when it functions immanently. Offering a sound moral argument in criticism of any one of our moral practices would be a matter of drawing upon insight from some other part of the moral life. It is in this fashion that reason in ethics is immanent in its employment. It is this immanence which is masked by the idea, which by now should strike us as very odd, that philosophy should be the foundation of a discipline of practical ethics, for there is no reason to expect that contemporary moral philosophy and philosophers are imbued with the kind of moral wisdom which would enable the discipline and its practitioners to distinguish moral insight from illusion. Indeed, the inveterate philosophical inclination to pursue the work of reason through the formulation of general principles and rules is bound to make the effort more an exercise in obfuscation than revelation. For the reasons given above, insight into these matters will not emerge at the level of a search for a principle which states what makes a being an item of moral worth. To cap it all, it is a mistake to suppose that debates about the adequacy of such principles really can escape close dependence on the moral judgements which emerge from our moral practices.

The handicapped and the human

The importance of reflection on the moral status of the cognitively disabled can now be underlined. The existence of these people among us challenges us to reflect on the existence of a range of practices and attitudes towards human beings which are revelatory of the special status of the human. They challenge us by the same token to reject the fundamentals of the methodology of popular styles of moral philosophy and the conception of reason they rely on.

The cognitively disabled challenge us to re-accept that there is a fundamental moral equality between us all, an equality which is not so much *based* on our natural equality as fellow human beings as *revealed* through recognition of our common humanity. The specific challenge they throw down is that of recognising that respect is due from me to the other human being as such regardless of what I may gain from him or her.

There is a tradition in writing on the foundations of people's sense of self-respect and self-worth in historical and contemporary moral philosophy which grounds an individual's awareness of respect and worth on his or her relatedness to others.[31] I am established in *my* eyes as a being who has moral standing by virtue of *others* treating my interests, concerns as things which affect their wills. Negatively, my presence in their path, their knowledge of my interests, will close off courses of conduct for them. They will not treat me as an object to be shoved about or manipulated as their desires dictate. Positively, they will act to help the satisfaction of my own interests. They will set store by my flourishing. It is important for my establishment as a being of worth in the eyes of others that my value for them is quite other than a use value. People might avoid harming and even cherish an object for the sake of the fact that they need it undamaged and running well for their own purposes. In this way an owner may see to the well-being of his slaves. But to come to a recognition of myself as a being of true worth through the behaviour of others, the forbearance and consideration they show to me must be unconditional.

Acting toward other human beings so as to establish in them a sense that they are things of unconditional worth enables them to grow up as beings with self-respect.[32] The demands thus created upon parents are strenuous. They are called upon so to care for others, their children, that they will be established as beings with a sense of having worth in their own right, independent of their value in parental projects and plans. The younger the child, the more care it will demand, the less it will be able to offer anything by way of supporting help and aid in return and the weaker it will be in its parents' hands. Family life and parenting are thus the occasion of significant moral challenge: the challenge of providing cherishing care which is unconditional and genuinely directed to the good of the other.

The cognitively disabled are likewise a challenge to unconditional care. As with children, the disabled bring to a head the demand that we place a value on others which is other than a use value. They can remind us that we need others to regard us as having a value which is not a use value. The disabled are thus a moral crux. How we treat them can tell us something about how we view ourselves. The more severely disabled they are, the more they cannot cover up their need for others. We may try to hide our need for others, a need founded upon the very roots of our existence as beings who need a sense of self-respect, but the disabled can 'remind us of the insecurity hidden in our false sense of self-possession'.[33]

For the various reasons explored in this chapter, I suggest we should see the cognitively disabled not as marginal persons but rather as central in our perspective of ourselves and of the moral life. They are treated as marginal from the standpoint of strands of contemporary moral philosophy – utilitarianism, pure and impure, and modes of contractarian thought. What reflection should show us is that these forms of moral philosophy occupy no Archimedean point from which they can survey the moral life and adjudicate on the worth of our practices. Rather than the arguments of contemporary bioethics weakening the perception that a disabled infant deserves and demands its parents' care, that perception shows up the pretensions of the moral philosophies we have criticised for what they are.

4
Euthanasia, Abortion and Genocide

Genocide and eugenics

The arguments offered by contemporary philosophers against the personhood of the cognitively disabled pose a particularly severe threat to disabled infants. The infant diagnosed as having a condition such as Down's syndrome is liable to be disqualified from personhood on two grounds: first, because infants as such are not self-conscious and rational; second, because the Down's infant's future quality of life is likely to be deemed insufficiently rich in these traits to make it even a potential member of the class of persons. Thus it is not surprising to find contemporary moral philosophers advocating the killing of such infants.[1]

The direct advocacy of killing cognitively disabled infants by the likes of Kuhse and Singer does not merely confront us with a theoretical problem. Such philosophical advocacy connects with the avowed practice of some paediatricians, who in effect take steps to ensure that certain infants in their care will die on the very grounds of the nature and extent of predicted cognitive (and other) disability.

The existence of medical practice directed toward killing cognitively disabled infants is demonstrated by a number of (in)famous legal cases which have attracted public attention in Western Europe and North America in the last two decades. The case of *Regina* v. *Arthur* will serve as an illustration of these.[2]

In 1981 Dr Leonard Arthur was charged with the murder of John Pearson (the charge was changed to attempted murder during the course of his trial) and acquitted on 5 November of that year. John Pearson was born on 28 June 1980 in Derby General Hospital. He was diagnosed as having Down's syndrome. His parents wanted nothing to do with him and indicated that they did not wish him to survive. Dr Arthur then put John on a regime of 'nursing care only', which implied that he was to be kept comfortable but given no food, only water. He also prescribed regular doses of dihydrocodeine (DF 118). The precise purpose of this prescription and the role of DF 118 in John's death on 1 July 1980 are subject to dispute. DF 118 is a pain-killer and a sedative. There is no evidence that John was in pain at birth. In one statement to the police Dr Arthur said its purpose was to prevent the child seeking sustenance. However, one of the expert witnesses for the Crown gave evidence to the effect that the dose levels found in John's body at autopsy were toxic and sufficient to kill him by depressing breathing.

Dr Arthur's acquittal turned around two things. In the first place there was evidence from defence pathologists pointing to undiagnosed physical defects in John Pearson. These may well have brought about the pneumonia which killed him, independently of the tendency to induce pneumonia of the starvation diet and drug regime on which Dr Arthur had placed him. Accordingly, the judge directed that the charge be reduced to attempted murder. In the second place, expert witnesses for the defence were allowed to argue that Dr Arthur's treatment of John was customary in many paediatric departments and thus fell within the bounds of a reasonable exercise of medical discretion. Crucially, the Judge, Mr Justice Farquharson, supported this view in his advice on the law of murder to the jury, affirming that Dr Arthur's policy was lawful if the infant was irreversibly disabled and its parents had rejected it. He further supported the defence witnesses' claims that there was an important distinction between 'letting a child die' through sedation and starvation, one the one hand, and actively killing it on the other.

The cogency of the verdict in *R. v. Arthur*, of the defence evidence and the judge's advice on which it was based have been the subject of intense debate.[3] Whether or not the verdict was legally sound, one thing is obvious: it is an affront to common sense to say that the treatment of John Pearson was not an attempt to kill him, but merely amounted to 'letting him die'. Leaving aside altogether the question of whether DF 118 in the quantities administered was or was not toxic, it is evident that the 'nursing care only' regime was designed to ensure that John never left Derby General alive. The policy behind the instruction of 'nursing care only' was aimed at bringing about his death. This much was indeed stated by the defence experts who testified to its use in other paediatric departments. The acts of omission in withholding normal nourishment from him were designed with a lethal intent in mind. The fact that they were omissions and not commissions is then not important. If I withheld food from my younger son in order that he should die, then I would have tried to kill him just as surely as if I had fired a rifle at him. The crucial question to be asked about the intent and purpose of the regime John Pearson had been placed on is this: what would have counted as its succeeding or failing? It seems evident from the context that the regime would have failed if by some miracle John had lived.

How far the paediatricians who spoke on behalf of Dr Arthur's decision to ensure John Pearson died represented a consensus as to good practice in British paediatric medicine is open to debate. A survey in 1981 of senior figures in the field showed little support for his course of action amongst those responding.[4] Yet, there is considerable evidence from other sources, including further legal cases and published papers by paediatricians, to indicate that there is a widespread practice of withholding life-saving care from the disabled new-born in order that they may die. Wolfensberger estimates that above 10 000 handicapped babies a year are killed in the USA by such methods, stating that 'widespread infanticide is now openly admitted in the medical community'.[5] I cannot vouch for the accuracy of his figures or his claim.

One thing is clear: some paediatricians take a prognosis of cognitive disability as sufficient for embarking upon courses of action designed to bring about the death of infants and children. We know this because some of the most celebrated cases involve Down's syndrome children. Down's individuals form the largest single group of the clinically retarded. They are particular targets for the medical policies under discussion because their typical physical characteristics are evident at a very early age and because they are frequently subject to digestive abnormalities, such as duodenal atresia (blockage in part of the small intestine), which, if not treated by surgery, will result in death. Many legal cases have arisen over the refusal by parents and/or doctors to give life-saving treatment to Down's children. It was in response to one such case of a Down's child (styled 'Baby Doe' in the legal battle surrounding him) denied surgery to overcome oesophageal atresia that the Reagan administration produced the so-called 'Baby Doe rules' forbidding Federally funded hospitals from withholding life-saving treatment and care from babies solely on the grounds of handicap.[6] The promulgation of the rules and the furore they created is some indication that Down's is taken by many paediatricians to justify lethal policies toward infants.

The facts documented in the literature on paediatric ethics and practice cause some writers to compare present policies toward the mentally and physically handicapped with those adopted by Nazi Germany. The Nazi genocide of groups such as Jews and Gypsies was preceded by policies of eugenic, medical killing which encompassed the mentally defective, amongst others. In all 275 000 people were killed as 'useless eaters' on the orders of Hitler.[7] The comparision with Hitler's policy of protogenocide can be made at a number of different points. Three points of similarity are claimed. First, a policy of killing handicapped new-born infants is widespread and systematic. Second, it is eugenic in aim, being based on the premise that those who are destined to be handicapped or of significantly below average intelligence deserve less of a chance of life than normal individuals. Third, this policy is bound to extend to destruction of groups of people who are generally unwanted or socially undesirable in the light of current standards. How far these points of similarity, and the general analogy between modern medicine and Nazi practice, can be sustained is a matter for debate.[8] The first alleged similarity has already been commented on. As to the second, whether or not there is a widespread policy of euthanasia toward the cognitively disabled, there are many individual cases which demonstrate a governing eugenic intent. The examples of John Pearson and Baby Doe show that the possibility of a child developing cognitive impairments in the mild to severe range is taken by some as a reason for the opportunistic withholding of life-saving treatment or for an early decision to snuff out life through a policy of deliberate starvation. The third alleged similarity is particularly contentious. It is based upon the claim that those who would take cognitive disability as a reason for 'letting a patient die' are on a slippery slope which, in the absence of a belief that all human life has intrinsic value, leads to dire consequences for anyone beyond the social pale.

The eugenic character of such policies fits in with powerful trends in nineteenth- and twentieth-century social thought which have seen the cognitively disabled as a threat to society and responded by endeavouring to ensure that the number of such people should be reduced for the future. Hence, we find in recent history the popularity of social isolation and sterilisation as measures to control the spread of 'defectives' in Western countries.[9] Some will link the endeavours to kill the likes of John Pearson with the widespread use of abortion following amniocentesis to terminate pregnancies where the mother is carrying a Down's foetus. Moreover, it is undoubtedly the case that these actions and policies are perceived as having a eugenic intent by the cognitively disabled themselves. Ann Shearer records the telling words of a disabled person who had attended a conference where the means of preventing disability were on the agenda: 'They want to get rid of us'.[10]

The lethal intent toward the infant disabled, encouraged by some philosophers and embodied in the actions of some doctors, suggests a contradiction in our society's attitudes to those with cognitive impairment. For that intent lives alongside active support for a growing disabled rights movement, which, in the case of the cognitively disabled, has properly insisted that such folk are people first and due the respect owing to all people.

The ethics of euthanasia toward infants with a prognosis of cognitive disability are inordinately complex. Even after we have stripped away the hypocrisy of saying that 'nursing care only' regimes amount merely to 'letting nature take its course', we are faced with the fact that many such decisions take place in the context of the neo-natal intensive care unit. The children involved may have many physical ailments and disabilities on top of predicted cognitive impairments. There may be real doubts about whether treatments or surgical interventions are worthwhile at all. No sensible person would want to give doctors an obligation to pursue futile and burdensome treatments regardless of consequences. Despite such complications, we need to separate out the ethics of practices directed toward eliminating children who are cognitively disabled. These will be practices based on the premise that the life-preserving care and treatment due to normal infants is not to be given to children like John Pearson on the sole ground that they are likely to have some degree of cognitive disability if allowed to live. Concentration on this issue will inevitably involve abstraction from real life cases.

The ethics of infanticide and of euthanasia

For the practitioners of bioethics discussed in Chapter 1 and Chapter 3 there is a special ethics of killing infants. 'Infanticide' denotes for them not merely a kind of killing, but a kind which is exceptional. This is because they hold to the 'threshold' view of personhood and place infants below that threshold. Thus, for the likes of Glover, the killing of a healthy, non-impaired infant is not the killing of a person and is not directly wrong. As noted above, on Glover's impure utilitarianism what makes such killing wrong, when it is wrong, is the violation it causes to the tender feelings of parents and the subtraction from the amount of future worthwhile life occasioned if the dead child is not replaced by another. I have argued against these conclusions. They can make no sense of the awareness which normal people have of the child as the focus of love. Their cogency in the context of philosophical reflection on personhood is doubtful once we see that the child and the adult it becomes are one being, one substance because they are one human being. To avoid the implications of this point, the defender of infanticide has to fall back on the implausible 'occasionalism' described in Chapter 3 whereby the object of value in a human being becomes his or her states of consciousness (or autonomous preferences) and not the human being as such.

If the arguments of the previous chapter are sound, then there is no reason to suppose that the killing of infants and children is governed by principles different from killing adult human beings. A lethal intent toward an infant will face as strenuous a demand for justification as a lethal intent toward an adult, for the fundamental fact about such an intent will be that it threatens a human being. The child-killer may indeed seem more heinous in his actions, since the child's innocence and helplessness adds to the plea it should make to justice and compassion.

The arguments of Chapter 3 make extensive appeal to what moral philosophers are wont to style our 'intuitions', but which, I have argued, are more properly regarded as fundamental ways of seeing ourselves and making sense of our moral lives. Kuhse and Singer mount what they take as a significant challenge to such an appeal in the ethics of infanticide. It is based in essence on a cultural relativist argument.[11] They state that many societies have in the past taken a wholly different attitude to the killing of children to that which now passes for orthodoxy in the societies influenced by the inheritance of Judaism and Christianity. They cite practices in the Classical world of exposing defective and unwanted babies in order to kill them. They argue that such attitudes toward infants are quite compatible with the establishment of a well-ordered community, which is otherwise in good moral and judicial health. Their aim, then, is to expose our 'intuitions' on the dignity and worth of the child as an historical blip arising out of a unique religious inheritance. Since most of us have abandoned that inheritance, we can surely abandon those 'intuitions'. In fact, infanticide carried out with parents' consent poses no threat to anyone in the community who is capable of realising what is happening – the threat to the victim is thereby disposed of.[12] The continued reliance on traditional 'intuitions' is equated with the 'totalitarian enforcement' of Christian ideas.[13]

The strength of this attack on customary moral attitudes has to be tested against a sense of the centrality of our perception that being a human being in and of itself gives someone a special claim upon us. On the account in Chapter 3 that sense is fundamental to much in our pattern of reactions to others. There is no more basic perception of another's claim upon us than the perception of that other's humanity. There is no deeper philosophical reason than the violation of humanity in the other which accounts for the horror of murder.

If the argument of the previous chapter is weak, that fact is not demonstrated by the cultural relativist reflections of Kuhse and Singer. The defender of humanity as something which is of central moral concern has a ready reply. The societies in which infant life was cheap were also ones in which other kinds of human beings were devalued, such as women and slaves. Precisely because they lacked the perception of the fundamental moral equality of all human beings signalled for us by Simone Weil, they present a spectacle in which all manner of distinctions were made among human beings, distinctions which put many types of human being beyond the respect of justice and the claims of compassion. We might on reflection regard our perception of the possession of humanity as the basis of respect not as a local prejudice inherited from a dark religious past, but as a hard-won recognition which we should cherish (we return to humanism as a moral outlook to be respected and deepened).

We can note that, where the moral equality of all human beings is not affirmed strongly enough, societies will create out-groups and classes of the oppressed whose members will then be treated as less than fully human. Ultimately, their lives will be regarded as cheap and will be cheaply taken. The out-groups will be formed of those who lack power and can easily be dominated by those who have it. It is a universal fact about human communities that they tend to create classes of devalued and deviant people whose lives and interests are taken to be cheap and not worth protecting.[14] One thing which a claim for humanity as the basis for a fundamental moral equality can do is to provide a standing bulwark against this tendency. Seen in this light, the thrust of Kuhse and Singer's arguments in *Should the Baby Live?* is clear: it is to make devalued groups out of infants and the handicapped (and a doubly devalued group out of the infant handicapped), so that members of these groups may be killed without compunction if the feelings of their parents and the interests of the wider community so dictate.

The notion of the moral equality of all human beings provides a clear basis upon which we can resist the efforts of those who wish to deny some of their fellows the due respect they are entitled to. Kuhse and Singer (and the other bioethicists who think like them) want to replace that clear basis with the concept of a life capable of displaying autonomy and self-consciousness and supported by a present desire to go on living. This new ethics of homicide thereby introduces the idea that there are some human beings whose lives are not worth preserving and whose interests are not worth protecting. This last thought is a dangerous one and inevitably raises questions about 'slippery slopes'. Can the key idea of human beings who have lives and interests less important than the majority be constrained in its application so that it does not lead to social consequences which even the hard-bitten utilitarian will find disastrous? We know that in certain circumstances this key idea can usher in corruption of moral and political sensibilities on a massive scale. The likes of Kuhse and Singer will claim that if this idea is constrained by the principle 'respect autonomous, self-conscious beings and their preferences for life and death', then it is harmless. Such reasoning depends on the thought that the concept of autonomous, self-conscious existence is precise and not open to elastic interpretation. But we may doubt whether the concept of a being manifesting autonomy and self-consciousness is precise. There is a significant penumbra surrounding the concept following from the fact that self-consciousness develops during early childhood and is manifested in primitive forms even as early as the end of the second year. There are adults who are reversibly comatose for significant periods of time following injury. Moreover, if what matters for individuals to be protected by rules forbidding homicide is that they display a self-conscious desire to go on living, then we have to cope with the fact that autonomous choice is exercised in a context. So, in considering how the ethics of Kuhse and Singer would apply to the elderly and long-term sick, we would need to be mindful of the many subtle and not so subtle ways in which choices can be influenced by the pressures of others. For these reasons, we may argue that there are grounds not to disturb our sense that there is something shocking in deliberately killing any human being. The preservation of such a sense defends us against the elasticity of the concepts moralists wish to replace it with.[15]

The defence of our sense that deliberately killing any other human being is shocking means putting the concept of homicide at the centre stage of our thinking about euthanasia. What is wrong with an act of deliberately starving a Down's baby to death is that it is an act of killing a human being. Our responses to killing indicate that the category of 'homicide' is a morally significant one. That a course of conduct is homicidal is a powerful reason in and of itself for regarding it as wrong and indeed heinous. An act amounts to murder if it is a homicide which cannot be justified as a homicide. Devine sums up this notion of murder clearly:

> Although not all homicides are murders, still that an act is homicide states a reason for regarding it as murder and hence as wrong. The conclusion that an intentional homicide is murder can be refuted, but unless a refutation is provided, the conclusion need not be defended.[16]

Making 'homicide' the morally significant category in this area of our moral life is a means of enforcing the moral equality of all of us. If the mere fact that an act is homicidal tends to make it murderous, if any homicide is murder in the absence of some justification for it as a homicide, then no further facts about the victim of the homicide need be cited to establish the presumption that killing him/her is wrong. By contrast, for Kuhse and Singer the fact that killing a human infant is an act of homicide is of no direct moral significance. 'Homicide' is for them a morally neutral category. Homicide is wrong in some circumstances, namely where it destroys worthwhile life as defined by their impure utilitarianism. In the absence of circumstances picking out some human victims (but not others) as worthy of protection from homicidal acts, homicides require no very strenuous justification. We have seen that this line of thought culminates in Rachels' comments on the killing of a severely cognitively disabled infant that 'there is nothing to be concerned with from a moral point of view'.[17]

If we accept the account of homicide and murder implicit in Devine's definitions, then we will have affirmed the moral equality of human beings in respect of their entitlement to protection by principles and rules forbidding murder. What Kuhse and Singer wish us to give up – when decrying the 'totalitarian' imposition of a Judaeo-Christian stance on the sacredness of all human life – is this thought about the moral equality of human beings. We will also abandon our use of the label 'homicide' as a morally significant one. In opposing them, we will be insisting that there is no difference *as such* between killing an adult human being and killing an infant. *Particular* acts of homicide toward adults and children may be distinguished from a moral point of view, but that will be a matter of specific facts about those different acts and will not follow from or track the fact that adults and infants are different kinds of human being. Customary distinctions among human beings made by reference to race, gender, age or physical or cognitive ability will not be relevant to any distinctions we make between the heinousness and acceptability of acts of homicide.

The thought that a homicide is murderous, and therefore wrong, unless justified as a homicide, takes us to a customary belief that an act of homicide requires a strenuous justification in terms which must refer to the victim of the act. Thus we might justify a police marksman's killing of a terrorist on the grounds that he was a potent threat to the lives and well-being of others. This seems to put arguments about what homicides count as murders in the territory of justice, insofar as to justify a homicide as a homicide we must appeal to facts about the victim which somehow show that his/her death was merited or deserved.[18] This connection between murder and homicide, on the one hand, and justice, on the other, provides an initial, albeit procedural, check against any genocidal social policies. They bid us ask how the members of those devalued groups merit or deserve the harsh treatment they receive. They make us ask whether mere membership of the devalued social or ethnic group shows that some deserve or merit death and make us interrogate the ideologies which seem to yield these conclusions. We have undertaken this interrogation into the quasi-utilitarian ideologies of Singer and others which suggest the conclusion that the severely cognitively disabled can be licitly killed.

The justice-based character of our reasoning about when homicide becomes murder should make us ask whether we can use economic arguments to demonstrate that a homicidal act is not really murderous and not really wrong. Therefore, if we accept the case given above for the centrality of the notion of homicide in our thinking about handicapped infants, we will hesitate to argue in the manner of Kuhse and Singer that the economic costs of not killing these children is a reason for legitimising their destruction. They point to the enormous economic and social resources which lifetime care for the severely disabled brings with it. They argue that these resources could be put to better use and conclude: 'There is a limit to the burden of dependence which any community can carry'.[19] Only if we accept the previous moves in *Should the Baby Live?* designed to make us abandon our categories of homicide and murder will this argument have any force. The economic costs of not killing someone cannot be set alongside the wrong of murder or make homicide justified as homicide. If shortage of resources for health care and social services tempt us to kill some infants that is the strongest reason possible to improve the allocation of resources in these areas. Economic reality is not fixed independent of human choices. The rich societies of North America and Western Europe could devote more resources to the care of the cognitively disabled without taking those resources away from other needy groups. These are matters of political and social choice, not hard and fast limits surrounding the human world.[20]

There is an empirical issue behind the appeal to economics to justify the killing of the cognitively disabled. Kuhse and Singer cite evidence to support the claim that improvements and developments in pre- and neo-natal care have resulted in a massive increase in children being born and surviving with significant combined physical and mental handicaps.[21] However, it is not so clear that the number of cognitively handicapped babies is increasing. The number of people with mild disability may be decreasing, measured against absolute standards of IQ, as improvements to diet, to general health and in environmental factors take hold.[22] There is evidence that the incidence of Down's syndrome among live births is declining, but that its prevalence is increasing as more Down's people survive longer into adulthood with better care.[23] None of this rather vague and ambiguous evidence suggests that the cognitively disabled present a major economic threat to our rich communities.

In extreme cases, it may be that the men and women running a neo-natal intensive care unit face circumstances analogous to triage: the resources available mean that they cannot treat all those presented for treatment and they have, in the contingent circumstances, to make decisions resulting in the death of some children. But if and when that does occur, it is a kind of tragedy and not something which should make us revise our views about homicide, children and the handicapped. In my view, it would be wrong in such circumstances to let the degree of predicted cognitive disability for an infant determine its place in any queue for life-saving treatment (save in the extreme case of disability to be discussed below). Tragic circumstances can be ones in which people are forced to do that which is evil. The revision to our understanding of killing advocated by Kuhse, Singer and others goes well beyond any considerations about the difficulty of avoiding homicidal decisions in circumstances of triage. It encompasses the thought that babies like John Pearson should not have their lives prolonged, because they are not yet persons, will have too low a quality of life according to some calculus and impose too great an economic and social cost on the rest of us. This is precisely *not* to see death-dealing acts toward these human beings as imbued with tragedy.

Not all homicidal acts are murderous. There are justified homicides. There are occasions when reasonable people, not simply those prejudiced toward the lives of children and the handicapped, feel it is right to authorise policies designed to bring about the death of infants facing a life of disability and handicap. Now, the arguments of bioethicists would have it that such decisions inevitably depend on the premise that the disabled have less worthwhile lives than the non-disabled. Frey makes this thought explicit when he makes judgements about the wrongness of killing a function of judgements about the value of that which is destroyed in the act of killing. If an act of killing is wrong it is because it destroys something of value; if it is licit, it is because it does not destroy something of value.[24] What is wrong with this claim, as Anne Maclean points out,[25] is that it makes the moral wrong in killing someone solely a matter of the natural good or evil resulting from the act. The thought that there might be something wrong *in the killing* over and above the end-state produced is lost. There is a further error in this utilitarian approach, an error which we have diagnosed above, namely that of taking the good or evil resulting from decisions to kill or preserve human beings to be a function of the amount of worthwhile life occasioned by the death or survival of the human being. This view does not take human beings to be objects of valuation, so much as see human beings as the occasion for, or vehicles of, bundles of experiences or interests. It is the satisfaction of desires and interests which is constitutive of value in the world.

No more space need be devoted to refuting the claim that stretches of 'life' rather than human beings are the real objects of value. The thought that in deciding that killing another is licit we are thereby ruling that s/he is of less value as a human being is equally misguided. The enemy soldier killed in a just war is of no less worth as a human being than anyone else. If we judge discriminate killing in a just war to be justified homicide, it is because of reasons bearing on the nature of this act, reasons which still respect the humanity of its victims. There is, for example, no contradiction in judging the killing of soldiers to be licit while mandating that the disarmed and wounded enemy are to be treated with humanity and compassion. The very general demand that exceptions to the rule that homicide is not to be done must be defended by something closely analogous, at the very least, to justice-based reasoning bears out the thought that licit killing is not based on denying the personhood of the victim. Exceptions must be based on reasons which explain how *this* person deserves to be treated differently from others. This procedure is one way of recognising what is due to the victim as a human being.

The following interim conclusion may now be drawn. If acts of euthanasia to handicapped infants are ever licit, then those acts have to be justified by reference to the same principles as homicidal acts to adult human beings (handicapped or not). Further, such acts have to be justified by reference to facts about the particular infants concerned which demonstrate why they deserve this discriminating treatment. Only if these requirements are met will acts of euthanasia toward the infant handicapped be compatible with respect for the humanity of its victims.

In the summer of 1981 a case came before the Court of Appeal which raised many issues similar to those present in *R. v. Arthur*. A Down's syndrome child needed life-saving surgery to correct duodenal atresia. Her parents would not give consent. They wanted her to die. Local social services sought advice from the courts as to whether the parents' refusal could be overridden. The Court of Appeal came down on the side of the child's life. In outlining his decision, Lord Justice Templeman offered the following rule:

> It devolves on this court in this particular instance to decide whether the life of this child is demonstrably going to be so awful that in effect the child must be condemned to die, or whether the life of this child is still so imponderable that it would be wrong for her to be condemned to die.[26]

As well as being based on a much more sensible estimate of the prospects for people with Down's, Templeman's reasoning points to the fact that there can, in extreme circumstances, be a case for euthanasia toward handicapped infants, a case which not only respects their worth as human beings, but is motivated by that very respect. This case is based on the thought that love and compassion toward the infant require that it not be allowed to live.[27] Killing of a handicapped infant may be judged to be in that infant's best interests and thus mandated out of respect for what is owing and due to the infant.

The argument that a 'best interests' criterion is the only one which will justify a homicidal intent toward the handicapped infant is mounted by Robert Weir.[28] It rests on the notion that some futures for individuals may be judged so horrendous that allowing those individuals to endure those futures is to visit a greater harm upon them than killing them or letting them die. Weir reasons about the situation of very severely handicapped and damaged infants by analogy with using death as a release from torture. If one knew that a person faced grievous torture for a long period and that the only means of escape from that future was to kill them, then homicide might be justified.[29] As a doctrine in medical ethics, Weir's argument gives pride of place to the principle of non-maleficence ('above all, do no harm') in the doctor's reasoning and invokes that principle in cases where the prognosis for a damaged infant is so poor (in the light of expected future pain, repeated surgery, institutionalisation, very limited capacities for a human-like life and so forth) that further life would be more harmful than death.

Weir's reasoning remains centred on the victim and employs considerations which might apply equally to adults and to children. Children are not relegated to sub-humanity by it. The reasoning thus meets the tests of acceptability proposed above. If reflection of this kind does treat the infant as a special case, it is only to the extent that we mark the suffering or degradation of children as particularly awful and as arousing our compassionate concern for their future in a special way.

A major objection to using a compassionate concern to avoid harm as a justification for euthanasia is that there can be no reckoning or estimate of the harm (or good) that is death. This objection is pressed by Devine.[30] There can be no rational choice for death or determination that death is a better outcome than living, argues Devine, for death is of its nature not a state of which anyone has any knowledge or experience. It is not even a state of myself which I could contemplate and compare with other possible states of myself; it is a condition in which there is no self to experience states. As a future, death is opaque and logically so. As against this argument, we must set the intuitive force in Lord Justice Templeman's reflections on some futures being demonstrably more awful than death. That is the thought that *whatever death amounts to* it cannot be worse than what we can predict will accompany survival. This thought need not present itself as a comparison between what two futures, both of which we can know and weigh. It is a sense that what is one side of the scale is so awful that the mere fact that what is on the other side will not include *this* makes the choice for the other side possible. Given that we are not comparing two states capable of independent estimation, Devine is surely right to point up the logical oddity of the judgement 'survival would be a greater harm to the individual than death', but I submit that he has not shown that such judgements are never compelling.

How will the compassionately motivated test of what is in an infant's best interests apply to euthanasia on the cognitively disabled? Well, we may note straight away that it will not mandate steps ensuring the death of an infant on the sole ground of Down's syndrome. With the leading analogy of the torture-victim in mind, no one can claim that the expected life of a Down's individual is so demonstrably awful that death is preferable. Much that we now know about the possibilities for Down's people encourages rather than discourages in viewing their prospects. Moreover, since the *variability* in developmental outcomes for Down's is well documented,[31] a death-implying prognosis for Down's children as such is doubly unwarranted. Where the best-interests conception will have immediate application is in those cases in which an expectation of future severe cognitive disability is linked to physical damage and handicap suggestive of future pain, medical interventions and the like. Meningomylocoele is one such severe physical condition with implications for cognitive development. And it is a condition which has resulted in paediatric practices which are euthanasiast in their intent.[32] Whether death-dealing in such cases is ever justified has to be judged in the light of the stringency of the best-interests test.

It might be argued that the best-interests justification of homicide has no relevance to the treatment of infants with a diagnosis of cognitive disability. For the fact is that cognitive disability does not appear to be painful or to occasion suffering as such. Thus, it might appear that it in the absence of any associated *physical* damage or handicap, there is no serious case for considering this kind of disability as invoking the possibility of euthanasia.

The best-interests justification of euthanasia will apply to the infants we are specially concerned with in this study if we adopt Ian Kennedy's 'critical criterion' of 'the capacity to flourish as a human being'. Kennedy locates the key to that capacity in the future ability of the infant to interact with others, 'to communicate, whether rationally through language or spiritually through displays of feeling and emotion' with other human beings.[33] Such a criterion does indeed engage with the case of infants who have a prognosis of profound cognitive disability. The problem with Kennedy's criterion is how to link it with the judgement that further life would be more harmful than death and the key analogy of keeping someone alive only that they may undergo a life of torment. How could a decision for death in Kennedy's kind of case be seen as moved by compassion and respect for the victim of our euthanasiast intent?

One way of linking the desires to prevent a life of future torment and to end a life with no prospect of human-like flourishing is as follows. The link is made via a thought about pain and torment which may be found to have some plausibility. The true evil of pain in a human being's life is not brought out by considering it merely as a disagreeable sensation. It rather lies in its capacity, if intense and/or prolonged enough, to take over the mind, to block out thought, to paralyse action – in other words to destroy all possibility of human flourishing. In support of this contention, we may point to the way in which some activities which give pain are nonetheless actively sought (think of the pain voluntarily incurred in struggling up a steep fell-side on a hot summer's day). Pain incurred within a chosen, worthwhile pursuit may be transformed into a positive experience. Pain which is not chosen, but which debilitates and fills the mind to the exclusion of all else is not a positive experience. It may be argued in this fashion that the root harm is that of a human being facing a future existence in which there is no prospect of partaking in any significant measure of human flourishing. It is this harm which, in extreme circumstances, may be regarded as so great that compassion and concern for the sufferer's interests mandate ending life.

The above argument about pain and flourishing may not in the end convince, in which case we are left with two unrelated criteria for judging someone's death to be in their interests. What is clear is that the case for the possibility of a choice for death for the disabled infant suggested in this chapter must face up to the worry that any such reasoning invites moral corruption. In my view, the way in which bioethicists write in favour of the killing of the cognitively disabled is a clear example of such corruption. The corruption enters in when a conception of what might be mandated by an appreciation of, and respect for, the humanity of the infant gets replaced by a concern for what suits others or what is best for society. The philosophical dogma that the disabled infant is not a person is but one mask for this corrupt swamping of the humanity of the child by concern for other people's (or society's) interests. To ward off such moral corruption we must bear in mind

Kennedy's affirmation of the 'amazing number of ways which humanity finds to express itself, despite apparently crushing difficulties'. This leads to his conclusion that 'the vote must ordinarily go to life' and his urging that the class of those who are 'marked for death' should be kept as narrowly and strictly defined as possible.[34] That the burden of proof lies strongly with those who would opt for death in such cases is something fully consonant with the thoughts about the nature of homicide developed in this section.

Kennedy's words are directly relevant to the case of Vicky, which has appeared in these pages before. Vicky – with a mental age of five months at 12, double incontinence and no ability to sit unaided – may seem a ready candidate for death. But her mother writes:

> That all paints a rather bleak picture but it's not as bad as it sounds. She is very pretty and very responsive. She is able to laugh, watches mobiles, likes musical toys and loves watching television. She also smiles when she hears a piece of her favourite music.[35]

Eugenic abortion

Wolfensberger regards contemporary Western societies as embarked upon a 'new genocide' toward handicapped people. A chief instance of this new genocide for Wolfensberger is the abortion of foetuses on the grounds that they will turn out to be handicapped at birth.[36] Evidently, these assertions depend on the equation of the morality of killing infants and adults, on the one hand, with the morality of the destruction of foetal life, on the other. The linking of foetal destruction on eugenic grounds with the devaluing of the disabled is cogent only on the condition that foetuses are regarded as human beings, or as having a status like that of human beings. With that view of the status of the foetus the conclusion offers itself that we are preventing the occurrence of disability by methods and on grounds which would justify destroying disabled people.

We know that many, many abortions are performed on eugenic grounds, that is: in order to prevent the birth of babies likely to be disabled. The two chief techniques of detecting potential disability applied to foetuses are chorion biopsy (chorionic villus sampling) and amniocentesis. Chorion biopsy is usually undertaken between the sixth and tenth weeks of pregnancy (that is, in the first trimester); amniocentesis is undertaken between the eleventh and eighteenth weeks (that is, in the second trimester). Both procedures incur an increased risk of miscarriage, a risk that is greater in the earlier test than in the later. In both, the risk of miscarriage means that it is normal to offer the procedures only to women with an increased chance of giving birth to a disabled child (for example, because of their age or because of a family history of disability). Both are primarily designed to reveal chromosomal abnormalities. So they are directly relevant to our theme, since conditions like Down's syndrome and fragile X syndrome are chromosomal in origin and productive of cognitive disability. But amniocentesis can also reveal conditions which are physically disabling as well, such as meningomyelocoele. It is routine in many places to offer mothers a termination if one of these conditions is diagnosed by such tests. Indeed, some writers assume that the elimination of Down's by mass screening via better and safer techniques of foetal diagnosis is a realistic and commendable goal.[37] While many forms of clinical cognitive disability, such as autism, remain undetectable by pre-natal means, the ethical issues involved in eugenic abortion are liable to be of still greater importance in future years. Research into the genetic background of conditions like autism and into pre-natal screening are areas of developing science. It seems reasonable to assume, then, that more pre-natal tests for more kinds of disability will emerge as science and medicine unfold.

A world without Down's people brought about as a result of mass pre-natal screening and routine destruction of affected foetuses: is this not an alluring prospect? Would it not be more alluring still to think of a world without any clinically-based forms of cognitive disability because all had become preventable by pre-natal diagnosis and abortion? Wolfensberger evidently thinks that to regard such prospects as desirable is at the same time to value negatively the existing people who are cognitively disabled. But perhaps this need not be so. We would all want to prevent the existence of people maimed by road traffic accidents. If promised a means of making transport on the roads utterly safe, we would take it. We certainly devalue the wounding and maiming that road accidents produce, but we do not devalue those individuals who live wounded and maimed as a result of such accidents. We can respect them as much as any human being, while at the same time wishing and working for a day when there are no more people with their particular afflictions. So: noting that people are afflicted and regarding their affliction negatively do not entail viewing those afflicted persons with disrespect. If people disabled after road accidents learn of strenuous efforts to prevent the occurrence of more victims, it would be inappropriate for them to complain: 'They are trying to get rid of us'.

I argued in the previous chapters both that it is sensible to regard cognitive disability as an affliction and that this does not at all entail regarding those who are so afflicted as any less deserving of the status and treatment due to human beings. Thus far, then, we may see no reason why we should regard campaigns of ante-natal screening to prevent cognitively disabled persons being born as implying disrespect to the disabled now alive. However, at this point Wolfensberger could urge a disanalogy with the campaign to prevent road accident casualties. He could argue: in trying to prevent the existence of this source of disability and affliction from occurring in the future, we are not contemplating destroying those who would be victims of accidents. In trying to prevent future cases of Down's syndrome, we are contemplating identifying those who would be Down's people and destroying them. Does not this stance involve more than the thought that Down's syndrome is an affliction to be valued negatively? Does it not involve the further thought that Down's people are a curse? Does it not involve valuing Down's people negatively?

This last point in favour of Wolfensberger's analysis of eugenic abortion to prevent the occurrence of cognitive disability has an emotive load to it. This load is present in the fact that the destruction of Down's foetuses is identified with destruction of 'them', the people who would otherwise be born later with the syndrome. It assumes both a continuity, indeed a numerical identity, between foetus and later human being. Further, an equivalence in moral status between foetus and later human being is posited. For the argument suggests that if we find a case for destroying foetuses who will develop into disabled people, that case will encourage us to regard disabled people as fit for killing.

The emotive load behind Wolfenberger's case does not seem so strong if we fasten upon instances in which advice about the risks of producing an afflicted child informs a decision not to conceive any such child. That way of preventing the occurrence of people with these disabilities does not appear to imply the same thought about the legitimacy of destroying them.

It is a desideratum of any sensible view of the ethics of homicide that it allows for a distinction between a decision not to conceive a human being and a decision to kill an existent human being. Normally, the decision to refrain from conceiving a child is not one fraught with moral significance (unless we hold strong views about the morality of various methods of contraception). Couples who, for one reason or another, incur a substantial risk of having cognitively disabled children may indeed face an agonising choice between the good of having or extending a family and the harm constituted by a substantive or increased risk of giving birth to a child with an affliction. But if they choose not to conceive any (or further) children, then their actions have no victims. No one is wronged by their choices. Their choices cannot then entail devaluing some victim of those choices. Thus, a sensible ethics will make a distinction between the non-conception and the killing of an infant. On these grounds, actual and potential steps to screen for clinical cognitive disability and adopt appropriate family planning policies is not part of a genocidal policy toward the disabled. Killing infants simply because they have or will develop such disabilities is. An ethics for abortion should fit the values which discriminate between an ethics for non-conception and an ethics for infanticide.

Thus far we have reached the following conclusion. To accept policies of non-conception in order to prevent the occurrence of cognitively disabled infants is not to endorse genocidal policies or attitudes towards existing disabled people. Wolfensberger's charge that routine terminations following pre-natal screening are tantamount to the acceptance of genocidal policies and attitudes remains to be considered. Accepting Wolfensberger's conclusion is equivalent, in the context of his overall argument, to accepting that destruction of the human conceptus (at least up until the gestational ages at which chorion biopsy and amniocentesis are performed) is the moral equivalent of homicide. In this way, the acceptance of routine terminations on the ground of diagnosed cognitive disability would be held to commit one to accepting routine infanticide on the basis of the same diagnosis. It is impossible in these pages to give a definitive answer to the question of whether destruction of the human foetus is the moral equivalent of homicide. There may be no definitive answer to give. However, it is important for our purposes to indicate that it is possible for someone who accepts Wolfensberger's condemnation of routine infanticide for the cognitively disabled to dissent from his equation of terminations of pregnancy, following chorion biopsy and amniocentesis, with a genocidal policy toward the disabled. Such a dissent to Wolfensberger's equation is possible for those who argue that, at least up to the stage at which terminations are typically carried out, the foetus is not a human being (or does not have the same moral status as a human being). There are at least two ways in which this conclusion can emerge: through a view which holds that a foetus does not achieve the status of a human being until it is born or through a developmental view of the foetus.

The view that humanity is achieved on birth is associated with traditional Jewish medical ethics. In that tradition it is rooted in scriptural authority. Exodus 24: 22–25 prescribes what penalties are due if 'men strive together' and cause harm to a woman who is with child. The verses distinguish between a fight which causes miscarriage in the woman bystander and a fight which causes harm (that is, harm to the woman). In the former case, a monetary penalty is payable 'as the judges determine'; in the latter case: 'you shall give life for life, eye for eye, tooth for tooth'. The passage is thus read as indicating that the foetus which has not yet emerged from the womb does not have the same status in religious law as a born human being. That status is achieved when the greater part of a baby has emerged from the birth canal (or, according to some authorities, when the head has emerged). Prior to that event, the destruction of a foetus is not taken to be equivalent to murder.[38] Some Rabbinic authorities have argued that the foetus is be treated as if it were a limb of the mother, at least before the process of birth gets under way.[39] None of this means that termination of pregnancy is devoid of moral issues for Jewish sources. Termination for trivial reasons may be considered gravely wrong just as deliberate wastage of the male's semen may be gravely wrong.[40] But a wrongful abortion does not partake of the wrongness of homicide. This stance allows Rabbinic authorities to license terminations well into gestation if they are backed by weighty medical, including eugenic, grounds.[41]

The kind of view of the attainment of humanity found in the Rabbinic tradition sees birth as a decisive discontinuity which prevents conclusions about the rights and wrongs of the treatment of children from being automatically read back into the treatment of the human conceptus. A developmental view of the status of the conceptus looks instead for a series of steps in the maturation of foetal life which cumulatively mark a gulf in status between the born child and the early conceptus. The developmental view may concede that there is an obvious sense in which the foetus is identical with the later human being, insofar as the human being grows out of the foetus. The foetus after implantation is a stable individual thing which in the normal course of development will become a human being. However, with this thought in mind, those who advocate the developmental view will claim that the very early human conceptus, prior to 14 days after fertilisation, is not one and the same thing as the later human being. This argument is based on the possibility of monozygotic twinning and, more generally, on the undifferentiated and unstable character of the material thing that is the early conceptus.[42] The argument can be extended. There is a discontinuity between the post-14 day conceptus and the later human being which can be pressed. One can argue that the foetus is not yet a human being but is rather developing into a human being. Something exists which in at least one obvious respect is not a human being. This respect is obvious if we take it that one way of using 'human being' is to refer to an organism with a characteristic anatomy, physiology and histology. In this respect, it is acceptable to say that the foetus is, for much of its development, not a human being but something which is in the process of becoming one.[43] It becomes a human being at the earliest around the twenty-fourth week of gestation when the fundamental metamorphic processes which turn the fertilised ovum into a being with our characteristic anatomy and inventory of organs are complete. The force of this way of looking at the relation between foetus and human being in the context of our argument about destroying that which may become a disabled human being is as follows. In this way the defender of abortion hopes to take away the sting of the objection 'But you are contemplating destroying *them*, that is, these disabled people'. What is contemplated is destroying some-thing which will or might become a disabled human being if left to complete the process of metamorphic development it is currently undergoing. Destroying the foetus prior to the completion of that process is not destroying a human being. It is not destroying *the human being* who will be disabled. It is not destroying a human being who exists now and is disabled. Destroying it is not an affirmation in action of the principle that human beings who are afflicted by cognitive disability may be licitly killed. So it is not part of a genocidal policy toward those individuals. It is fully consistent with the contrary principle that human beings with these afflictions are to be valued and respected as we value all human beings, because they are human beings first and afflicted second.

Establishing either the Jewish or the developmental view of the humanity of the foetus as a reasonable possibility suffices to show that objecting to routine infanticide for the cognitively disabled does not commit one to rejecting pre-natal screening and terminations altogether. Both views are naturally subject to argument and objections, but both can be said to square with some common reactions and attitudes. People tend not to regard the natural destruction of a zygote or embryo as the equivalent in human life of the death of a child. Miscarriage at a very early stage of pregnancy is undoubtedly the occasion of distress. But many would find it odd to grieve over the embryo. By contrast, we could all understand a couple who wished a proper burial for a stillborn, premature child. The other side of that understanding is a natural feeling of unease, to say the least, at the remains of foetuses from late, third trimester abortions simply being incinerated. They have a human shape and form.

It is a desideratum of any sensible view of the ethics of homicide that it allows for a distinction between a decision not to conceive a human being and a decision to kill an existent human being. Both the birth-centred and developmental view preserve that distinction. So will a non-developmental view which fastens upon conception as of decisive moral status, but such a view must of course endorse Wolfensberger's strictures on eugenic abortion. There is no sense in which this study is committed to any one of these three positions. Nor have we said anything by way of giving advice to couples presented with the choice to abort foetuses diagnosed as likely to develop into cognitively disabled infants. It would be presumptuous to give such advice. Decisions of that kind are properly left to the consciences of the individuals concerned. To make that point about conscience is a way of marking the fact that there is no proof of a *right* way of deciding whether abortions in such cases are licit or not. Why then has space been devoted to outlining different views of the status of the conceptus? One reason is: some might contend that it is so obviously the case that eugenic abortions to prevent cognitively disability are routinely licit (if not mandatory), that there must be something wrong with the account of infanticide defended in these pages. It is important to rebut that charge by showing that there are at least defensible accounts of the moral status of the conceptus which avoid having to transfer an ethics of abortion into an ethics of infanticide. Another reason for outlining alternatives to Wolfensberger's governing assumptions is that much legal regulation and public opinion (I do not say *all*) in effect implies those alternatives. There is a sense in much law and opinion that abortion is always a serious matter, the choice of which stands in need of regulation and the backing of reasons, and that the later in gestation a choice for abortion arises, the stronger those reasons must be. There is also a sense that the licitness of abortion is a separate matter from the licitness of infanticide. The creation of a legal licence for abortion does not entail a similar licence for child killing. That combination of views can provide a way of framing a social policy on abortion in the absence of agreement and proof on the moral rights and wrongs of the matter. A birth-centred or an evolutionary view of the moral status of the foetus can contend that aborting a foetus close to the end of gestation on eugenic grounds partakes of the seriousness of infanticide on such grounds, whereas the ethics of aborting an earlier foetus does not need such a strenuous justification.

There is no common sense view of the ethics of abortion and the above remarks are not an attempt to provide one. The major contention of this section is negative: reasonable individuals are not bound to see aborting foetuses likely to become children with cognitive disabilities as the moral equivalent of a genocidal policy of killing infants because they will develop such disabilities. Wolfensberger's contention that the two policies are mutually equivalent is based on a particular view of the human conceptus, to which reasoned alternatives are available.

However, even those who do not share Wolfensberger's tacit stance on the moral character of foetal destruction may still argue that the key contentions of this section provide too easy a response to part of what is at the root of his complaint about abortion and the disabled. Both the decision to prevent the conception of a cognitively disabled child and the decision to abort an early foetus on these grounds are based on a common thought: it is better that there be no such people as the cognitively disabled. Such measures prevent impairment by preventing the birth of impaired people. Now, though these preventative measures might be agreed not to be the equivalent of homicidal acts, it is still the case that they exhibit an attitude found in those who advocate the killing of infants with a prognosis of cognitive disability. The attitude is that, in the absence of a 'cure' which will rid a person of disability, it is better not to have such people at all. Preventative family planning and abortion are based on the premise that if we consider the worth of a human being with this kind of affliction, we must judge their lives to embody so little net value that we should not allow such people to come into existence. What is this but to endorse the perception of these kinds of disabled people as an out-group, as a curse and a burden upon the rest of the population? Matters are worse in the specific case of terminating a pregnancy on these eugenic grounds. Regardless of whether the foetus which is thus destroyed is or is not a human being, it is still the case that we contemplate destroying a something which will develop into a person with disability on the very grounds that it is better not to have such persons.

These criticisms might be strengthened by pointing to an alternative to eugenic family planning and abortion. This is the notion of the conception and birth of a human being as a gift. An authentic attitude toward a gift does not seek to judge the worth of what is given or to reject those gifts which we would not welcome. The notion of the birth of a human being as a gift is most at home in a context of religious ideas about grace and providence. A view of this kind is anti-eugenic in its thrust. It is a perspective which might seem more suited to the idea that handicapped people are to be valued just as much as other people.

The above objection needs to be taken seriously. It takes us back to the problem with the analogy which has shaped discussion in this section: trying to prevent the future occurrence of people maimed in road traffic accidents does not imply devaluing the extant victims of such accidents, so preventing cognitive disability does not imply devaluing extant people with these impairments. But in the accidents case, we prevent the occurrence of the maimed people by preventing the accidents. In preventing these disabilities by way of contraception and abortion, we are preventing the conception and birth of the people who might otherwise exist with the disabilities. We are not preventing people getting these disabilities.

While the above objection should give us pause, it is not clear that it is decisive. We have sided with Wolfensberger's affirmation of the injustice of making the cognitively disabled a devalued group. We have done so because it fully coheres with the leading principle of this study: Simone Weil's claim that respect is due to the human being as such and is not a matter of degree. We have interpreted this claim to consist in recognising a range of fundamental obligations of justice, non-maleficence and benevolence which are owing to these disabled people in the same way and to the same degree as they are owed to anyone. For the objection to be finally telling, it would have to be shown that there was some contradiction or tension in affirming both the Weil claim about the moral equality of us all and the desirability of policies in the area of contraception and abortion designed to prevent cognitively disabled people being born. I cannot see that contradiction or tension, because the Weil affirmation is based on the perception of another as a human being in my midst. That perception is sufficient to generate the further perception of moral claim and equality. But if it is proper and just not to perceive sperm and ovum (and perhaps the conceptus at some stages of development) as another human being in my midst then the Weil affirmation is not to be invoked.

We might test our judgements on these matters by considering how things stand when we ponder the prevention of pervasive physical illnesses. Suppose that diabetes were preventable by screening of parents and by screening the conceptus in its early stages (accepting, for the sake of argument, that the early conceptus at least is not a human being). So through contraception and early termination the birth of people with the condition could be prevented. Would the adoption of these measures commit us to attitudes toward existing diabetics which implied that they were devalued, second-class human beings? We would indeed be saying that we should prevent the birth of people who, if they existed, would have diabetes. But those who have diabetes are people in our midst and as such are not second-class human beings, because there are no second-class human beings. All are morally equal. We need not be saying to the diabetic human being in front of us: 'It would have been better if you did not exist'. This is because the 'you' refers to an existing human being and that thing is the locus of a special value just in being a human being. We might appropriately be credited with the thought 'It is better that we prevent the occurrence of human beings in the future who would have diabetes'. But that is not to devalue any individuals with diabetes, because it does not refer to any individuals. It does not say of a number of non-existent, future human individuals that it is better that we don't create them. Non-existent, future human individuals are not individuals. In this fashion, it does not entail any statement of the form 'It would have been better if *you* did not exist'. It does not refer to any human beings in our midst.

To recap: if we agreed with the policy of preventing the birth of people with diabetes through contraception (or early termination), we would be saying that it is better that we do not have future individuals who have the property 'suffering from diabetes'. The crux of my argument is that this is not the same as saying of some individual human beings (in this case: possible, future human beings) 'It is better that you should not exist'. So it does not entail judging of other individual human beings (actual people with diabetes) 'It is better that you do not exist'. We can speak about future, possible people by mentioning properties which future individuals could or could not have. But an individual is not just a collection of properties and our speech about future individuals does not refer to individuals. The properties we mention when we discourse of what future people might or might not be like ('having diabetes', 'being autistic' or whatever) are not properties of individuals who happen just not to exist yet. There are no subjects in which they inhere waiting to traverse the boundary between possible existence and actual existence.[44]

The substance behind what might seem to a critic to be a metaphysical quibble is this: we rest on the absolute premise that being an individual human being suffices to make someone a possessor of the kind of moral worth which rules out their being a fit object of genocidal policies. That premise is not shaken or disturbed in any way by policies and acts designed to prevent the coming into existence of human beings with certain kinds of afflictions, because the objects of those policies and acts are not human individuals. The human individual who has, say, the property of suffering from a cognitive disability cannot lose the moral status that comes with being an individual human being. Having that property of impairment constitutes the individual as an afflicted human being, who, as such, is deserving of remedial help and care with a view to maximising his/her chances of partaking in human flourishing. To act so as to prevent the existence of individuals in the future who have this property is not in and of itself to affirm or imply that there are any actual human beings who are to be deprived of the opportunity to partake of flourishing.

The critic of the limited defence of the thinkability of eugenic abortion for cognitive disability may feel that part of the point behind Wolfensberger's strictures has been neglected hitherto. The response to Wolfensberger has been defensive. Arguments have been offered for saying that those who properly condemn genocidal policies toward the disabled new-born are not forced thereby to condemn eugenic abortions. Perhaps what moves Wolfensberger is the worry that once society comes to regard such abortions as licit, it will rapidly move to regarding them as *mandatory*. If society generally thinks no wrong of the order which invokes the rule 'do not do evil that good may come of it' is involved in abortion, it will *expect* couples to terminate pregnancies where there is a chance of disability. It will expect even more strongly that contraception should be used if there is the slightest indication of a genetic risk of disability. The upshot of this will be that cognitively disabled persons will increasingly come to be seen as mistakes: people who should not have existed if matters had been properly ordered. Moreover, their parents will be seen as folk who have wilfully brought suffering and cost into the world. Intolerance toward the cognitively disabled will grow and Wolfensberger's strictures against genocidal policies toward existing disabled people will be under ever greater strain.

The above argument deals in the long-term consequences of routine screening and termination for cognitive disability. It is impossible to tell whether these predictions will come true. It is clear that if we say decisions about termination after screening are down to individual conscience, then we allow that some couples may legitimately feel (in the light of their views about abortion) that there is an evil done in termination so grave that it may not be done for the sake of the harms it prevents. Such conscientious judgements are to be respected. We are not without resources to prevent the dire predictions coming true. The humanist stance defended in this book should be a bulwark against any devaluing of afflicted people, or reluctance to devote material and human resources to aiding such people. Moreover, even if fewer couples produce disabled infants in the future, there will still be very many injured, disabled and damaged people in society who will keep our sense of compassion and justice alive.

There is something deeper on which reflection is needed before we close this chapter. I have taken it that cognitive disability is to be seen as an affliction. How much of an affliction it is depends naturally on the severity of the disablement. That means it is something we should, crudely, try to fight and to eliminate. No parent of a disabled child would properly eschew remedial therapies which lessened a child's cognitive disability or that disability's handicapping character. I draw the following consequence from this point: a parent who had no qualms about the licitness of the means (such as contraception or abortion) involved should opt where possible for the prevention of the occurrence of a child with a disability of this sort. There would be a kind of irresponsibility in opting for the production of such children, unless one did have doubts about the means which had to be used to prevent that outcome.

The above point is a delicate one. It is the case that very, very many parents of cognitively disabled children regard them as significant pluses in their lives. It is easy to descend into sentimentality in expanding on that thought. But we can say that though such children take and they cost, they also give and what they give can often be astonishingly rich. So, overall, the lives of their carers can be enriched by their presence, and enriched in ways not available in nurture of the normal child. Notwithstanding that point, we should take all licit means to prevent the future occurrence of the cognitively disabled (as we must to prevent disablement through traffic accidents or to prevent diabetes). I regard these conclusions as further adumbration of the main theme of this section: it is right to regard cognitive disability in the abstract, in isolation, as negative in value, but it is right to regard the concrete whole who is the child (the person) with the disability as of intrinsic, compelling worth.

5
Cognitive Disability and Oppression

If we cannot bear to see when someone needs *different* provision verbally and practically we will all end up being stupid.[1]

The cognitively disabled as an oppressed group

There can be no question that the cognitively disabled have been an oppressed group in the history and recent past of our societies. Members of the group have stood out as different from the normal population. That in virtue of which they are different – diminution of species-typical capacities for communication, learning, social interaction and executive planning – has made them devalued as human beings. There are two aspects to this oppression, as there are to the structure of oppression wherever we find it: the concrete ways in which the oppressed have been treated and the set of attitudes surrounding and reinforcing those modes of treatment.

The first aspect of oppression could be described and illustrated endlessly. In the industrial societies of Western Europe and North America we find in the recent past a common history of the segregation of cognitively disabled people. This segregation has gone hand in hand with systematic policies denying them any semblance of civil rights and any share in the common good. Segregation has meant incarceration. It has meant denial of the opportunities for meaningful education and work. It has also meant denial of the right to marry, enjoy sexual relations and procreate. These forms of mistreatment have been supported by the second aspect of oppression: a fundamental attitude of disrespect and devaluation toward those impaired in cognitive powers. In sum, the cognitively disabled have been treated as a classic out-group. We have seen the ultimate expression of this status in the Nazi attempts to kill them, an expression which finds its echo in contemporary attempts to justify the destruction of cognitively disabled infants.

The character of the injurious treatment of the cognitively disabled in modern Western society can be gleaned simply through reading the testimony of those segregated and institutionalised in the recent past. Frank Thomas's account[2] of his treatment in British 'hospitals' for the mentally handicapped can only make one ashamed that a society allegedly built upon respect for the principles of humanism could systematically subject members of a vulnerable group of people to degrading and inhuman treatment.

The past failure to give cognitively disabled people help in personal and social development, in education, training and employment betrays a lack of justice as well as an absence of compassion toward them. They have effectively been cut off from participation in the common good, where that means a reasonable opportunity to partake of the basics of human flourishing. That they have been neglected, where they should have been helped, may be explicable simply through the natural egoism which stifles compassion and makes us seek justice for ourselves and those with whom we can identify. But the segregation, incarceration and maltreatment of the cognitively disabled are only fully explicable through the fact that they have been perceived as a positive threat to society as a whole. The nature of this threat is illustrated in the much-quoted remarks of the American Social Darwinist Walter Fernald to the Massachusetts Medical Society in 1912:

> The feeble-minded are a parasitic, predatory class, never capable of self-support or of managing their own affairs. The great majority ultimately become public charges in some form. They cause unutterable sorrow at home and are a menace and danger to the community. Feeble-minded women are almost invariably immoral, and if at large usually become carriers of venereal disease or give birth to children who are as defective as themselves.
>
> We have only begun to understand the importance of feeble-mindedness as a factor in the causation of pauperism, crime and other social problems. Hereditary pauperism, or pauperism of two or more generations of the same family, generally means hereditary feeble-mindedness. . . .
>
> Every feeble-minded person, especially the high-grade imbecile, is a potential criminal, needing only the proper environment and opportunity for the development and expression of his criminal

tendencies. The unrecognised imbecile is a most dangerous element in the community.[3]

These thoughts are extreme but not untypical of the once widespread view that the cognitively disabled are a threat. They have been perceived not merely as people who are incapable of participating in human flourishing and the community, but as a danger to others. No doubt some of these attitudes and the practices they engender are explicable through the presence of false beliefs (about, for example, the sexuality of the cognitively disabled, their criminality and the easy heritability of the conditions which produce disability). Yet these attitudes toward the cognitively disabled cannot be solely explained through intellectual error. The errors are too egregious, the attitudes too widespread in many human cultures and epochs for such a diagnosis to be sufficient. Moreover, there is an obvious correlation between such attitudes and policies, on the one hand, and deep human needs, on the other, which cries out for further explanation. To see that correlation we need to turn to the character of oppression as a psycho-social relation.

We must confront the question of what it is for the majority or the dominant in a community to create out-groups and why the existence and oppression of such out-groups is so widespread a feature of human social life.[4] A leading theme of this study is Simone Weil's claim that equality of respect is a deep need of the human soul. Such equality of respect stands under constant threat from the structures of human power.

Human beings exist within a network of power relations. They find themselves exercising power over others or being the subject of power exercised by another. Power relations can arise and exist with legitimacy but there is an inevitable tendency for them to become exploitative. The non-exploitative relation will be structured by a continued recognition of the other human being as a creature worthy of respect. Structured in this way, the power relation will be limited. Power relations so limited provide a standing affront to the egoism of individuals and groups. There is a natural tendency to seek recognition and deference from others by exploiting their relative weakness, by forms of overt or covert coercion. Non-coercive relations with others cost.

Coercive, exploitative relations between powerful individuals or groups and weaker individuals or groups are inevitably paradoxical, since they are a manifestation of a kind of weakness in those who coerce and exploit. It is the weakness displayed in the inability to accept others as moral equals and a consequent inability to see those others as beings who can return respect and standing freely and fully. Paradoxical or not, there is a natural tendency for human beings as individuals or members of groups to seek to confirm themselves as beings of worth by coercing and exploiting those who are weaker.

The coercing of out-groups embodies a moral psychology whereby worth depends not on the presence of humanity as such, but on the possession of some favoured characteristic possessed by the powerful and lacking in the weak. A discriminatory scale of human worth can operate alongside the coercion of others, if those coerced constitute an out-group defined precisely by the lack of the discriminatory feature. A psychology is created in which the oppressed are encouraged to judge their worth by the lack of the feature which the oppressing have. Oppression then acquires a double edge. The oppressed are liable to devalue themselves (and therefore seek less for themselves) through being partners in the dominant moral psychology. The oppressing are by contrast confirmed in their self-image and power by the same discriminating value system. The psychology enforced by the discriminating value system is anti-humanistic. It denies the equality of all in terms of moral and personal respect which derives from common humanity and which is non-discriminatory. Power is used to create, and is in turn buttressed by, a discriminatory value system in which the qualities of the powerful define the basis of respect and worth. Such a value system must provide a way of hiding and/or defusing the fact that the oppressed are human beings and share that humanity with the oppressing.

In sum: out-groups of oppressed people exist in human communities because of the fact that inequalities of power naturally arise in those communities and because of the tendency of power relations to become morally corrupt. The moral corruption has one important source in the cost of maintaining a respect for oneself and others which is based on mere and common humanity. Oppression is maintained through a discriminatory, comparative value system which reflects the privileged character given to the features unique to those who are the agents and beneficiaries of oppression. These value systems are binary: worth is defined through possession of the traits of the dominant group and lack of these traits is sufficient for lacking worth.

The cognitively disabled are the victims of a widespread and seemingly convincing discriminatory value system. They lack to some degree or other species-typical traits of cognition. They are devalued because they are deficient in these traits. In many instances they can be identified as different at a glance. That the cognitively able have devalued them on these discriminatory grounds has been a way in which the able have confirmed themselves as beings of worth in their own eyes. Not to devalue the cognitively disabled, not to make an out-group of them, entails a cost which many human beings in many cultures have found, and continue to find, too great to bear. It is the cost of accepting that shared humanity, something without possibility of enforcing discrimination within the human community, is sufficient for worth. We are here positing a fundamental difficulty in individuals and communities accepting that the basis of worth can only be non-discriminatory and that power relations must be limited by a recognition of the universal possession of worth by human beings. In this respect, the remarks of Fernald represent a universal human tendency to create out-groups, a universal dynamic of oppression and a standing temptation (from the nature of the case) to make the cognitively disabled a target of these tendencies. The contemporary case in bioethics against the personhood of the cognitively disabled can be seen as an endeavour to rationalise this universal tendency and this standing temptation.

It follows from the above analysis that there is a mixture of universal and particular factors explanatory of the practices and attitudes of modern industrial societies toward the cognitively disabled. The practice of segregation in large institutions is clearly contingent on wealth and organising power of a certain kind. The fact that these institutions came to be styled 'hospitals' and were under medical control reflects the contingencies of the growth of medicine in modern society and the rise of its prestige in social life. Much of the rhetoric in the quotation from Fernald is determined by the intellectual fashions of his day. However, the analysis given above, plus the points in Chapter 3 derived from Edgerton's cross-cultural studies of cognitive disability, suggest that we will find that the cognitively disabled will be marked as an out-group and treated accordingly in many societies. As noted in Chapter 3, we should therefore be wary of those accounts which tell us that it is owing to industrial capitalism and its demands for disciplined, quick-working factory hands in great numbers that ill-treatment for such folk arose.[5] We have seen that it is false to claim that in non-industrial communities cognitively disabled individuals were invisible and easily integrated into patterns of work.[6] The harsh treatment that has been meted out to the cognitively disabled in our societies may be contrasted with tales of peasant communities where they are treated as saintly or touched by God.[7] But we can equally find many non-industrial communities in which such folk get heartless, harsh treatment.[8] We have seen how the moral psychology of the human being and group, reinforced by the logic of power, encourages comparative modes of judging the worth of human beings. Moreover, it is an undeniable fact about deficiency in, or lack of, species-typical cognitive powers that it will make it difficult in many instances, if not impossible, for the people concerned to contribute economically to the community. Such deficiency will tend to establish dependence upon others and mean that the cognitively disabled are economic burdens. Being 'problem-engendering' in this way, the cognitively disabled will be a natural candidate for discriminatory attitudes and treatment.

Labelling and oppression

Having briefly surveyed the existence and dynamics of oppression toward the cognitively disabled, we must return to a question broached in Chapter 3: does the very act of drawing a distinction between 'them' and 'us' by means of a label such as 'mentally handicapped', 'mentally retarded' or 'cognitively disabled' promote oppressive attitudes and treatment toward the people so labelled? Now we must confront the case that the category so created is bogus because it is the agent of oppression.

Before looking at the arguments in the literature for the above claim about the oppressive content of the concept of cognitive disability, we need to make some obvious points of clarification. The statement that 'the concept of cognitive disability is oppressive' is a 'nothing but' one. That is to say, it is meant to provide a reason (conclusive at that) for disallowing present use of that concept. Given that, it must rule out the possibility of noting that, while *some people* have used the concept or its equivalent (compare Fernald on the 'feeble-minded') to express oppressive attitudes and justify oppressive treatment, a redeeming, non-oppressive use of the concept and its associated distinction is after all perfectly in order. The concept is nothing but a moment in an oppressive mode of thought. This entails further that there is some form of modal claim within the statement about cognitive disability and oppression. The modality in the statement must be something to the effect that it is not possible to use the concept without committing oneself or encouraging others to regard the people so labelled as unworthy of fundamental respect. Put this another way: the claim must be that it is a necessary condition of using the concept or taking it seriously that one have an attitude of disrespect, of devaluing, toward those who fall into the category – which is to say of course that use of the concept is sufficient to commit one to such an attitude. It cannot be that any such 'deconstruction' of a concept through giving its 'genealogy' in past, oppressive thought simply notes that some, or even many, people have used the concept as part of an oppressive system of thought. Without an argument establishing what we are *committed to* in using the concept, such an account lacks bite. After all, there are many concepts innocent in themselves of pejorative or oppressive entailments which have figured in discriminatory attitudes. That many have taken concepts like 'woman' or 'foreigner' to pick out grounds for devaluing other human beings is no reason for abandoning them, since they can be used perfectly well without such overtones and are needed for legitimate purposes. Recall the structure of the thought that leads to 'cognitively disabled' or its equivalent being an agent of oppression. We have an in-group, with power, defining itself through the possession of various traits. It uses its power and these traits to define, ill-treat and dominate an out-group which lacks these traits. We have, fundamentally, a failure to see that mere humanity is sufficient for respect and the replacement of that non-comparative standard of worth with a discriminatory, comparative one. So, the mere noting that there are traits which some have and others lack, and which therefore enable us to put human beings into different classes, is not sufficient for oppressive attitudes to exist. The noting of the presence of such traits in some and their absence in others is not therefore sufficient for oppressive modes of thought to arise. The fundamentals of the moral psychology we have described must also be present. In those who recognise the moral equality of all human beings, for whom the presence or absence of traits like being white, male, Anglo-Saxon and of normal intelligence is irrelevant to fundamental moral worth, the mere noting of differences between one's self and others is no encouragement for oppressive attitudes. Those who argue that the mere noting of differences, as between the cognitively able and the cognitively disabled, must entail the dynamics of oppression appear to share the premise that if there are important natural differences between human beings, they must be the grounds for different degrees of moral standing. Hence, they appear to share part of the moral psychology which produces oppression. Only because they see no alternative to that moral psychology, must they deny the reality of important natural differences between human beings. Within the outlook we have derived from Simone Weil, natural differences between human beings are not denied. They need not be because the basis of moral standing – mere humanity – trumps those differences.

There is a good reason why the Weil outlook will want to seek and mark differences between human beings. Committed to the moral equality of all members of the species, it will want to give all an opportunity to share in human flourishing. It will note that some human beings have afflictions which mean that they need the aid of others to acquire that opportunity. It is an important feature of any community committed to the Weil outlook that it will want to help its weak, vulnerable or afflicted members. Thus it will want to mark out children from adults and treat them differently because children need special treatment if they are to develop into human beings who flourish. It will want to mark out the sick for the same reason. Likewise, it will want to mark out the cognitively disabled. This will not be a way of marking them out as non-human or less than human, but rather as human beings first, human beings who need special help in their development and aid in their adulthood if they are to have a chance of sharing in human flourishing.

If the above case for saying that 'cognitively disabled' and its equivalents do not have to be oppressive in meaning and function is sound, then it follows that the arguments from 'critical theorists' aiming to deconstruct the concept will be weak. This is in fact what we do find.

It is possible to discern in the literature a rough and ready case for the dismissal of the concept of cognitive disability on social and ethical grounds. The four main theses of this deconstructionist case against the concept of cognitive disability are: (i) there is no scientific and hence objective basis for the distinction made by the concept; (ii) the concept in some sense creates the phenomena it seeks to pick out; (iii) the concept serves the ends of those professionals appointed to educate or treat the cognitively disabled; (iv) the labels associated with the concept swamp recognition of the humanity and individuality of those to whom they are applied.

These four theses amount to applying a hermeneutics of suspicion to the way in which the cognitively disabled are described and treated in our societies. It is essential to this hermeneutics that the reasons given for categorising, describing and treating the cognitively disabled be unmasked as mere rationalisations. Thesis (i) is thus essential to the enterprise. It must be shown that there is no objective basis to categorisation and description in this area. Hence, we find Bogdan and Taylor arguing that the 'scientific aura' of a term such as 'mental retardation' is 'deceptive' in that it serves as a cloak for moral and cultural value judgements.[9] In fact 'Labelling and testing provide a cloak of scientific legitimacy to social control and oppression'.[10]

Bogdan and Taylor's evidence for thesis (i) is drawn from the failure of IQ tests to give a decisive, culture-free and non-relative measure of mental deficiency. We have explored the force of this point in Chapter 2. We may concede that a good deal of writing in this area has been cloaked with a false air of scientific rigour. It is also the case that the putative 'science of intelligence' has been linked with eugenic and Social Darwinist thought nakedly political in its intent.[11] But the lack of any science of intelligence does not at all entail that there is no objective fact of cognitive disability, nor does it entail that science cannot tell us much about such disability. There is, we noted in Chapter 2, no accurate, scientific measure of where cognitive disability is present and absent. That no more entails that the distinction is subjective than the lack of an accurate, scientific measure of happiness entails that there is no distinction between an individual sunk in misery and a normally happy one. And even if science cannot provide a measure of intelligence and its lack (because it is not a unitary phenomenon capable of measurement), we have seen that science can provide much valuable information about conditions such as Down's syndrome and autism which tend to produce cognitive disability. What is objectively present behind the category is the fact that there are species-typical powers of cognition which are important for the functioning and flourishing of human beings as language-using, adaptive, social creatures and that a small minority of the species lacks some or all of these powers to a degree which is significant enough to give them serious problems in functioning as individuals and as members of the community. The argument of Chapter 2 above was that the absence of a global science of cognitive disability does not entail that there is no fact of disability independent of the prejudices of the majority. It just is the case that a minority of human beings, illustrated by the young autistic child who cannot speak at five, present themselves with major deficits in cognition. What is true is that what counts as such a deficit is relative to a context, namely that of the typical powers and capacities required to function as a human being in a social setting.

In presenting thesis (ii), critical theorists move from the premise that the category of the cognitively disabled is without objective foundation to the natural conclusion that it is a human, social invention. Those aiming to deconstruct the category of the cognitively disabled seem to wish to deny that some human beings really do have major impairments which would be present regardless of how a society chose to regard them or treat them. Bogdan and Taylor again illustrate this move. In a series of rhetorical sweeps they claim that a classification of some as 'severely and profoundly retarded' (in scare quotes to imply that these people are only so-called severely and profoundly retarded) is a self-fulfilling prophecy. If we assume that such people cannot learn, then they will not learn – because we will not teach them. Schools fail children and the blame is put on their retardation.[12] Caroline Gooding quotes with approval the claim that the process of labelling a child as one who has impairments produces the special child rather than anything which the child may have within him or her, there being (it is implied) no pre-existing category of children with impairments.[13]

This part of the deconstructionist case shows the influence of the social reaction theory of deviance. According to this theory, deviant behaviour in human beings is in large measure created by the process of social labelling of the deviant and the consequences of that labelling. Forms of deviance, such as mental illness, cognitive disability and criminality, are fundamentally social roles. Individuals who exhibit these forms of deviancy may have exhibited some prior, primary deviancy, by for example acting in a way which is contrary to current social norms and expectations. But the main component of their deviancy will be the secondary deviancy resulting from them being placed in the social role of the deviant. The social reaction to primary deviancy may include being labelled in a certain way and being incarcerated against the deviant's will. Once labelled and managed by society, the behaviour of deviants will come to conform to the pattern laid down by society's definition of the role they now occupy. If they are placed in institutions like asylums or hospitals for the mentally handicapped, the control over their behaviours will be total and they will be surrounded by people also acting out the social role of the deviant. On the social reaction theory, then, deviancy such as cognitive disability is in the main socially created and manufactured, for people will react to how they are treated, to what is expected of them and in accordance with the behaviour of others around them. The theory imputes a motive to the social creation, through labelling and institutionalisation, of secondary deviancy.

Labelling and its consequences are forms of social control. Primary deviancy which is felt to be threatening to the social order can be handled by the labelling process. Primary deviancy exhibited by the weak is the means whereby society maintains control of behaviour and lifestyles contrary to dominant social norms. As a secondary effect, the social creation of secondary deviancy creates powerful professional groups who thereafter have a vested interest in maintaining the existence of groups of clients labelled deviant.

It is this set of ideas which govern Jane Mercer's dismissal of the reality of all but 'pathological' cognitive disability which we met in Chapter 2. Her case culminates in the following claim:

> If a person does not occupy the status of mental retardate, is not playing the role of mental retardate in any social system, and is not regarded as mentally retarded by any of the significant others in his social world, then he his not mentally retarded, irrespective of his IQ.[14]

I take the force of this claim to be that, if it were not for the enforced placement in the social role of retardate by others, the cognitively disabled person would be unimpaired. At least in the majority of cases (that is, for the 'mildly' mentally retarded), impairment consists in nothing other than being placed in a social role and suffering the consequences thereof.

The social reaction theory of deviancy was prominent in the anti-psychiatry movement of the 1960s and 1970s, and its application to the cognitively disabled is due in some measure to the influence of that movement. It is a key claim of the anti-psychiatry movement that the labelling and treatment of some people as 'mentally ill' in large measure creates the behaviour which professionals then claim to be able to manage. It is assumed that Foucault and others have shown that madness is a socially created role, a role linked to the need to control forms of primary deviance which threaten the social norms and power structures of late-capitalism. Yet these ideas in anti-psychiatry have not stood the test of critical examination, not least because there is ample evidence to demonstrate that very many of those who come to be labelled and treated as mentally ill have exhibited symptoms, which they and their families have noticed full well, prior to engagement with society's institutions for classifying and managing mental illness. Moreover, these people's symptoms are disruptive and painful to themselves and their immediate family. They gain contact with the professionals and institutions dealing with mental health voluntarily, because they and their families suffer through their primary deviance. They are, in the typical case, in touch with professionals and institutions for a relatively short proportion of their lives, are frequently helped by those professionals and institutions to overcome their primary, distressing deviance and face no permanent stigma or social devaluation because they have had contact with the world of mental health.[15]

Sociologists concerned to test the key claims of the social reaction theory of deviancy have found little evidence to confirm, and much evidence against, the key claims of the theory and their application to cognitive disability.[16] The child who is autistic, Down's or whatever will present with delays in normal and vital functions (such as speech and learning) before any contact with institutional systems, and their labelling processes, is made. It is hard to give any credence to the thought that their problems increase after their contact with institutional systems, or that their main difficulties in flourishing as human beings are created by their non-voluntary assumption of a social role.

It may be objected on behalf of thesis (ii) that when we turn to past attempts to mark out and treat non-clinical, 'socio-familial' mental retardation there is force in the idea that labelling and treating the cognitively disabled as such creates their problems. Consider the workings of the Mental Deficiency Act of 1913 in England and Wales as a typical example of the way in which an advanced industrial nation dealt with many people who had no pathologically caused form of cognitive disability. The Act gave a central board of control and those acting for it legally backed power to detain in hospitals people deemed mentally defective. Its effect was to produce a massive increase in the numbers of those with mild cognitive disability detained in institutions. Studies indicate that half of those detained came within the normal range of intelligence as measured by IQ. Brian Kirman concludes:

> In fact those admitted under the 1913 Act were those without families, the destitute, the unemployed, the illiterate, those without homes, those who, usually in the case of men, had engaged in petty pilfering or similar offences or who in the case of women had become illegitimately pregnant or were accused of soliciting or had similarly offended against the law. . . . Often the category of feeblemindedness

has been used to cover persons of dull to average intelligence with a poor scholastic record who presented something of a social problem.[17]

So there is a genuine history of labels such as 'mentally deficient' and associated institutions being used as a means to deal with social problems, rather than to help the people caught up in the labelling process. In Chapter 2 we noted that the mechanisms of IQ give a false impression of objectivity to the diagnosis of people as 'retarded' in this way. Many such people have in the past been classified on the basis of IQ by institutional systems (particularly the education system) only to become socially invisible once free of the influence of such systems. There is a significant penumbra surrounding the category of the cognitively disabled. Real deficiencies in species-typical powers provide the key criterion, and not merely failure to conform to dominant social expectations. The fact behind the labelling is that some children and adults who need help to function as human beings typically do because their cognitive powers are impaired. Society should otherwise be capable of accepting a wide variation in people's social behaviour or their ability to gain from, or be successful in, formal schooling without diagnosing the presence of disability. It is perfectly fair to charge that in the recent past, if not in the present, industrialised societies have regarded and treated those who would not conform or were not adept at formal schooling in a prejudiced manner. Labels such as 'mentally deficient' have been part of that prejudicial treatment and have been integrally linked to too narrow a view of what it is to be a human being.

Thesis (ii) claims that the category of the cognitively disabled is socially created. According to (ii), being cognitively disabled is a social role some are forced to play, but there is little, or nothing, problematic in the life and being of the people so categorised apart from the fact that they have been categorised. I have contended that this key claim is plain wrong if we consider clinical forms of cognitive disability. It has a grain of truth when we reflect on the reality of some people classified as retarded or deficient in the past who suffered from no organically related impairments. But even where there are no such organic impairments, it may be evident that people are cognitively disabled prior to their coming into contact with professionals and institutional structures. So there is a class of individuals with genuine primary deviancy, deviancy which is not created by the construction of social roles.

If thesis (ii) is true, there is no category of people out there needing help from physicians, psychologists, educators, speech therapists and the like. Thesis (iii) then comes into play. The category of the cognitively disabled and its neighbouring categories (child/person with learning difficulty, and so on) must be created for the benefit of those professionals whose careers and whose power depend on 'helping' those placed into the category. The institutions run by these professionals must exist to serve their own ends and not the ends of their clients.

The above claims have been pressed at length and in detail in relation to the institutions of special education and the categorisation of children as having the learning difficulties making them fit to become clients of those institutions. Sally Tomlinson's *A Sociology of Special Education* has popularised these ideas about special education. Crucial to her case is that special education is not in truth designed to meet the needs of its child-clients, despite the rhetoric of 'children with special educational needs'.[18] There is a general need in a late-capitalist society for a compliant, productive and educated workforce. That society confronts the fact of a minority of children who are nonconformist and troublesome, relative to its standards. Special education exists in order compulsorily to exclude these children from ordinary schools so that compliant children can be educated in accordance with social expectations. The fiction that there is something inherently wrong with the excluded children helps the late-capitalist society marry its systematic and compulsory exclusion of such children with its avowed commitment to egalitarianism.[19] The economic interests of society at large then enmesh with the vested interests of the professionals who manage special education and gain a status and living from such management. Their theories about the special child, their activities in classifying such children, provide them with a client-base which keeps them in business. At this point Tomlinson's theory can link in with a postmodern deduction from the writings of Foucault to the effect that 'all knowledge is power'. That is to say, what passes for expertise, for knowledge, is generally the unwitting means of creating and preserving the power of some group or other, the institutionally or professionally organised set of people who manage that 'knowledge'.[20] It is part of Tomlinson's overall aim to denounce as ideology the 'benevolent humanitarianism' which has officially motivated the institutions of special education. This ideology grounds the institutions on the mandate to help children who have special needs, whereas the institutions are really there to serve the economic needs of society at large and the vested interests of a variety of professionals.[21]

Tomlinson's main target is the use of the concepts and institutions of special education to deal with children who, in English terms, were traditionally classified as Educationally Sub-Normal, that is, as having problems coping with formal schooling which could not be traced to some *further impairment* such as autism. So Tomlinson concentrates on those styled as 'disruptive' or as 'slow learners' rather than on those with what she calls 'normative handicaps'.[22] Let us leave aside her claims about those without 'normative handicaps'. What concerns me most of all is the impression that such an account of the ideological and self-serving function of special education can be applied to, or has important lessons for, the education of children with diagnosable cognitive disabilities. Thus Caroline Gooding moves from noting the argument of 'critical theorists' that categories distinguishing the special child serve social control in a late-capitalist society and the interests of powerful professionals to include in this critique, via association, the creation of new categories for disabled children: ' "aphasic", "dyslexic", "autistic" . . . all of which children were recommended for "special" education'.[23] The implication here is that these categories do not correspond to anything in the children so labelled. We can concede to Gooding that there might be some truth in the claim that some aspects of the structures of special education do not serve the real interests of children (but then no human institutions are free from defects). We can also concede that the human business of creating concepts to mark out disabilities is prone to error and sometimes has little science behind it. Notwithstanding these points, those who have to care for children with cognitive disabilities will regard it as the height of stupidity not to acknowledge that the real world contains many children who require special schooling. They require it because they have real impairments in cognitive functioning, which, if not attended to, will cut them off from doing many of the basic things other human beings can do: things like speaking, relating to others, coping with novelty, reading and writing. If they are lucky, they will live in a late-capitalist society which has generated sufficient surplus wealth to enable them to get this special help. If they are lucky, there will be people prepared to work long hours with difficult children (for not very much money) and who are dedicated to maximising the personal potential of those they look after. The implicit claim that such work is self-serving and not an expression of active kindness guided by genuine skills requires strenuous justification.

Of course it is true of some institutions that they grow so as to benefit those they employ and not those they supposedly serve. Of course it is true that many of the institutions which catered for the cognitively disabled in the recent past were dustbins not serving their clients' best interests. Of course it is true that the category of the cognitively disabled has been used to sweep up too many people and place them in those dustbins because social and educational institutions for the majority were too narrow and rigid in their expectations. But all of this argues for greater care in using the notion of the cognitively disabled and better treatment for those so diagnosed. These points are not a sufficient argument for treating the very idea that there are cognitively disabled people who need special treatment as corrupt and oppressive. If we abandon the label and the caring institutions which properly go with it, we will have cut off a significant minority of human beings from aid and help which they need. Some so labelled in the past were no doubt thereby harmed. Their liberty was denied them. Their right to take a place in the community was not honoured. But, if we dismiss institutions such as special schooling as there merely to serve the needs of professionals, a corresponding great harm will result to those who genuinely need professional help and care.

Thesis (iv) in the deconstructionist critique suggests that, whatever the utility in having a category of the cognitively disabled might be in other directions, labels such as 'mentally retarded' or '. . . handicapped' are stigmatising and therefore should be abandoned. This may simply be the complaint that these and other terms have acquired too many negative connotations over the years for them to be safely used now. They have, it may be argued, become the inescapable vehicles of prejudicial attitudes. Taken in this way, thesis (iv) might simply be a terminological one: a proposal to mint a new term such as 'learning difficulty' which does not have established, traditional connotations of a negative or dismissing kind. Thesis (iv) seems relatively trivial when so interpreted. As a substantive thesis it is much more likely to rest on the thought that to name anyone or any group via concepts and labels which denote a lack of something deemed positive or beneficial is inevitably stigmatising and therefore oppressive.

Goffman defines a stigma as follows:

> an attribute that makes him [the stranger, the other] different from others in the category of persons available for him to be, and of a less desirable kind – in the extreme, a person who is quite thoroughly

bad, or dangerous, or weak. He is thus reduced in our minds from a whole and usual person to a tainted, discounted one.[24]

It can easily be argued that 'cognitively disabled' or its equivalent has functioned as such a stigmatising label in our societies, as the remarks from Fernald quoted above amply demonstrate. In particular, the classification of someone as intellectually disabled has functioned as an all-pervasive one, 'all-important and all-permeating, overshadowing other abilities, talents and characteristics',[25] with the result that it has been impossible for people so classified to escape from the stigmatising effects of this label. The label has implied nothing less than total lack of worth as a person:

> mental retardation . . . implies moral inferiority as well as intellectual deficiency. . . . To be called retarded is to have one's moral worth and human value called into question. It is to be certified as 'not one of us'.[26]

Thesis (iv) clearly reflects some of the ways in which labels have functioned in this area. The question is whether they must so function and whether to give them up is not in fact to endorse the corrupt modes of thought which are productive of stigmatisation. We need to note straightway that the perception of others as having an inferior-making stigma is not dependent on the use of labels. The fact that people's appearance, behaviour and speech are markedly different from the normal is very likely to produce the stigmatising reaction and invoke the dismissal of their personhood by the ignorant, the foolish, and the prejudiced. Parents of cognitively disabled children rapidly become used to them being stared at and looked over as if they were from another planet. It is possible to feel in the eyes and reactions of others, particularly of other children, the stigmatising effect. It is not people's responses to words that we need fear most in this area. But, it may be objected, there is no reason to provoke further the stigmatising reaction by labelling via terms implying deficiency. The response to this is that to avoid terms indicative of deficiency, disability and impairment on these grounds is to give in to the very dichotomous conceptions of human worth which are at the root of these problems. The description of someone as cognitively disabled can only be a means of calling into question their moral and human worth in the operative conditions of a mode of valuing human beings which depends on taking the traits possessed by the majority to be necessary and sufficient for value as a person. To reach a point at which the moral equality of all human beings has been accepted will involve our being able to recognise someone as afflicted, impaired and disabled without that recognition at all implying a judgement of worth. To accept that calling attention to others' defects is inevitably stigmatising is to accept a binary, comparative mode of valuing as the standing condition for viewing ourselves in relation to others. We should, on the contrary, constantly challenge those modes of valuing. We can do so by forcing those who think in these terms to face the fact of impairment and difference in others while getting them to accept that this fact has no morally significant implications. By these means we challenge, continually and vigorously, the binary, comparative mode of valuing which has been so disastrous for the cognitively disabled. In this light, the fashion for the anodyne 'person with learning difficulties' may appear to be a timorous concession to past modes of valuing, rather than a new, bold step toward equality.

The responsible use of speech must be sensitive to context. There may be contexts in which the use of labels such as 'cognitively disabled' is not appropriate, in which it is, for example, better to side-step, rather than challenge directly, the mass of moral prejudices governing the thought of those with whom one is in dialogue. And we must concede that 'person with learning difficulties' may be a useful label in such contexts. It may help to remind the prejudiced that the disabled are like everyone else: human beings with some limitations.

But for the final point against thesis (iv), we must return to a comment which led us into this discussion of the four-part deconstructionist case. Those who are advocates for the cognitively disabled will need words which draw attention to their difference from the majority of the population because they will be pleading for special treatment for these folk. To give them what is owing and due to them as human beings – an opportunity to partake in the basic human goods – will be to plead for them to have more of society's resources than others. For these purposes, we will precisely *not* want many of the cognitively disabled to be invisible members of the community. We will want to draw attention to the range and depth of their special needs (something which 'learning difficulties' will not do unless it becomes part of a code, signifying more than it literally means). We will want those special needs to be in the front of the minds of those who plan educational, health and social provision. Being special in various ways and being specially in need of resources are not incompatible with, but rather follow from, the equality the cognitively disabled share with all human beings. What is owing to them as human beings entails these costs, because of their impairments and afflictions.

There are some things which those who advocate the deconstruction of the category of the cognitively disabled and I can agree on. The disabled have been maltreated in the past and continue to receive less than their due as human beings in the present. It is wrong to justify such maltreatment by supposing that being disabled entails a loss of moral status. Being disabled does not entail loss of moral status at all. Where the deconstructionists and I disagree is that the very creation and labelling of a class of people with these disabilities is the root of these errors. Rather, I have argued, their root lies in wrong attitudes supported by the distorting effects of power on human consciousness. But, though words can encourage and justify prejudice, it is not *words* (labels) that we need to fear and to combat most in defeating prejudice.

Segregation and normalisation

The effects of social reaction theory of deviancy show in an assumption which many advocates of the disabled make about the relation between the disabled and society: any form of segregation or creation of separate institutions for the disabled harms them. Ann Shearer in *Disability: Whose Handicap?* offers us an example of this assumption at work. She contends that the primary handicap the disabled suffer from is that created by the social response to their initial impairments.[27] This point is evidently a variant on the theme that primary deviance is less important than the secondary deviance which is socially imposed. The handicap faced by the disabled, for Shearer, is a function of the inability of society at large to create environments which allow human beings with other than the normal run of physical and cognitive abilities to engage in fulfilling human activities. Handicap is thus the result of the failure of society to adapt to the full range of the manifestations of the human, rather than a consequence of the mal-adaptedness of the disabled. One of the primary means by which society reinforces its refusal to adapt social environments to the disabled is through the exclusion of the disabled from those environments. Separate institutions thus function to harm rather than help the disabled. They are the means by which society's narrow image of the human is preserved and by which the disabled are confirmed in the role of disadvantaged, unwanted persons. There can be no adaptation of society to the disabled unless there is recognition of the disabled as human. Segregation is a barrier to recognition. So, for example, special education for the physically and cognitively disabled is the means of handicapping them in the long run.[28]

I do not wish to discuss Shearer's main thesis on disability/handicap at any length. We have noted in Chapter 2 that the notion of handicap is a relative one. Recognition of the disabled as human is called for. It should entail that we work harder to adapt the social environment to the needs of the disabled. How far the Shearer thesis successfully copes with the handicapping nature of severer forms of cognitive disability is much more open to question. Of central concern at this point in the argument is the claim that segregation of the cognitively disabled, as in special education, is in their long-term worst interests.

The segregation claim applied to separate, special education for the cognitively disabled can be expanded upon by drawing upon social reaction theory once more. It may be argued that segregated schooling cuts the cognitively disabled off from appropriate role-models. Children segregated in these ways will be thus encouraged by their school environment to acquire socially inappropriate behaviours. These behaviours will make it more difficult for them to adjust to social life outside school. The effect of being sent to a special school will in itself be to label the child as an underachiever. It will also serve to stigmatise the child in the eyes both of the 'normal' children in its home environment and in the eyes of its teachers. Teachers when confronted with a child labelled in this way will have lower expectations for its development and will act accordingly. The child will react to these lower expectations by lower achievements. The segregating, labelling and stigmatising processes establish a mutually reinforcing, vicious, downward cycle, which will all too often leave the student fit only for work and life in more special institutions and segregated workplaces after special education is complete. The model to be adopted should rather be that motivating the US Education of All Handicapped Children Act of 1975 which mandated that disabled children should be educated in the least restrictive environment and alongside their non-disabled peers to the maximum extent appropriate.[29]

The attack on any kind of segregated educational, social or occupational provision is also found in Wolfensberger's version of the goal of normalising life for the cognitively disabled. According to this version of normalisation, what is vital for the future of the cognitively disabled is that they should be enabled to 'pass' (in the terms of Goffmanesque sociology) in everyday society. This means getting them to behave, and having them treated, so that their primary deviancy, whatever it may be, will be invisible so far as is possible to normal society. Hence, they will avoid the stigmatising and other effects of the labelling process. The disabling and handicapping effects of secondary, socially created deviancy will not be able to take hold. As part of allowing the cognitively disabled to 'pass', service provision should seek so far as is possible to integrate them fully into normal society. This aim will be defeated if they are given institutional care which marks them out as filling the socially devalued role of a cognitively disabled person. What is crucial in the lives of the cognitively disabled is that they have been, and are always liable to be, subject to a negative social evaluation. Separate, segregated institutional provision can only confirm that negative social evaluation.[30] The correlate of these ideas is the closing of special institutions for the cognitively disabled, the greater readiness to have disabled children cared for at home and the general move to 'care in the community'. These moves have of course paralleled similar trends in the treatment of the mentally ill.

If the criticisms of the social reaction theory of deviancy outlined in the previous section are sound, then much of the intellectual basis for the attack on separate institutional provision for the cognitively disabled vanishes. If we accept that primary deviancy (that is, cognitive impairment) is the most important source of disability which cognitively disabled people face, then the social effects of institutional provision will be less important than the impact of that provision upon the primary deviancy in question. Thus, for example, we will be open to the following kind of unfashionable suggestion: should institutional placing of a Down's adolescent with a severe degree of cognitive disability enable greater personal development for that individual, it is to be preferred to that person continuing to live with his/her family in the community. On this alternative view, the chief failing of institutional provision in the past has been its *quality*, following from its failure to see that efforts to help the cognitively disabled develop intellectually and socially are capable of reaping great dividends.

Sue Szives' powerful case[31] for the possibility of separate, segregated provision for the cognitively disabled starts from the premise that the most important goal of their education and treatment should not be the fostering of a better image of them by society as a whole but should rather be developing and securing their sense of well-being. Like other human beings, their sense of well-being will depend upon appropriately supportive and rewarding relations with other human beings. But these are not necessarily to be found by integrating them with the rest of the population. They may meet hostility and ostracism there – negative reactions not created by labelling but by a perception by others of their primary deviance. They may compare themselves with others, the normally endowed, and gain a negative self-image as a consequence. They may need space to behave differently from the mass of the population without attracting attention thereby. They may need to foster a group identity. People can be in the community, in the sense of being geographically in it, while also being isolated from it through lack of friends and acquaintances. In order to encourage appropriate self-esteem and well-being, we may well want the disabled to be different and that in turn may involve encouraging them to be separate from the mass of the population.

One upshot of the above counter-case against Shearer and Wolfensberger is the welcome some writers give to the creation of special communities for the cognitively disabled, such as the Camphill villages in Britain and the L'Arche communities in France. In such places a lifestyle may be developed which allows a fuller approach to normal human flourishing than is possible by living in the community. This is to encourage society as a whole to accept that there are different ways of being human through accepting that there can be plural, separate lifestyles.[32] Seen in this light, Shearer's and Wolfensberger's rejection of separate and segregated provision for the cognitively disabled can be interpreted as another attempt to impose others' views about what is acceptable and appropriate in the way of human living upon those who may have quite other views themselves and, even if lacking such views, may not be benefited by the imposition.

The counter-case to Shearer and Wolfensberger having been made, we can return yet again to the case of special education. It has been noted that there is a contrast between the espousal of integrated schooling on the part of professional educationalists and advocates for the disabled, on the one hand, and the surge by parents of the cognitively handicapped to seek and indeed set up special schools for their children, on the other.[33] Why this parental demand? One reason is that many parents of children with cognitive disabilities seek special schooling after very poor experiences with mainstream education for their children. They feel that their children can flourish best in a school environment which is tailored to their unique needs and capacities. At best, a mainstream class is always going to be an environment which compromises between the needs of their children and normally endowed children. Above all, they may feel that their children are going to develop to the maximum extent only through the provision of specialist help. This will be available where there are many professionals and small classes. A concentration of children with a given kind of disability, such as autism, can justify specialist therapists permanently attached to the school (such as speech and language therapists). A concentration of staff allows for the better dissemination of skills among them all (thus if one teacher gets intensive training in a specialist teaching skill, s/he can pass it on to others). If specialist equipment is needed, it is more likely to be provided if there is a group of children who need it.

Overall, parents may feel that the special school provides a much more prosthetic environment for their cognitively impaired child. If their child has spent time in a mainstream class, they may have found that its primary impairments led to its being ridiculed or ostracised by other children and the encouragement of a sense of failure and inadequacy in it.[34] By contrast, in the special school the child's impairments will be accepted. They will form no barriers to the child being a valued human being in the eyes of the school community. Thus the special school will provide the best kind of supportive base for the child's exploration of community life. They will reject the argument that labelling a child (as 'autistic', 'aphasic', 'Down's' etc.), lowers teachers' expectations of its development and thus harms it.[35] They will instead be impressed by the dedication of teachers in the contemporary special school to the philosophy of seeing the possibility of development in all children and seeking the maximum development for each.

The rival propositions that integrated schooling is better for cognitively disabled children and that integrated schooling is worse are not susceptible of strict scientific proof. Strict proof of either proposition would only be available in the impossible circumstances of comparison of educational and personal outcomes after random assignment of cohorts of disabled children to mainstream and special schools. Assessment of how children develop in the different systems without randomisation will always be subject to biases in the samples. We could not be sure that one cohort had no more primary impairment to overcome than the other.[36] But no responsible educational body or group of parents would agree to a randomised trial of this sort. In this respect, the arguments for either of these propositions function at the level of common sense and personal experience. However, I hope to have done enough here to show that the case mounted by Shearer and others against segregated schooling does not triumph on intuitive or common sense criteria.

The attack on segregation and special institutional provision for the cognitively disabled loses its intuitive power once we turn our attention to the individual, his/her primary impairments and possibilities for development. With such a perspective, the reaction of society at large to cognitive disability is apt to seem less important to that individual's flourishing. What will assume pride of place is the means by which the effects of primary impairment can be overcome through specialist help and/or mitigated through special, prosthetic environments. It was this attention to the individual disabled person which was at the heart of the Scandinavian pioneers of normalisation for the cognitively disabled.[37] What struck the likes of Nirje and Bank-Mikkelsen as normal about the cognitively disabled was they have, in all but the most extreme cases, the capacities for personal development and for a sense of well-being possessed by all human beings. These capacities were not being developed and catered for in previous institutional patterns of care and education. Segregation, as in special schooling, need not be opposed to normalisation understood as the drive for personal development and a sense of well-being for the cognitively disabled. Segregation can indeed can be motivated by the ideals of normalisation.

Justice and flourishing

As noted in the preceding section, past patterns of care for the cognitively disabled in advanced industrial countries have not been good. Such people have been seen as a threat and incarcerated in institutions designed largely to keep them out of society's way rather than to develop them as human beings. These institutions have even, in some cases, served to remove from circulation persons who were merely socially undesirable but with no diagnosable or significant disability. In the last three decades, all this has changed. The change is marked by new slogans and models: deinstitutionalisation, self-advocacy, normalisation, mainstreaming. There has been a demand for care directed toward personal development, not social exclusion.[38]

The changes have not merely been rhetorical. New patterns of care and education for the cognitively disabled have emerged. But these changes have created a problem. The cognitively disabled and their parents and carers have become petitioners for resources. Understandably, they do not see the demands for special educational, housing and employment provision as fit only to be met out of charity, but rather as societal obligations to be discharged by the state and its agencies. In the role of petitioners for more and more state resources, the cognitively disabled and their carers come into conflict with other groups seeking aid from the public purse. Such conflict then raises the general question of what claim the cognitively disabled have on society as a whole. What is owing in justice to these people? They are only a small minority of the population yet they demand special provision which will be expensive, both in terms of financial and human resources. The problem is highlighted in an example at the start of Henry Veatch's discussion of justice for the retarded.[39] An education authority has a finite budget. Should it spend large sums giving a severely retarded child the special education it needs to develop minimally in the direction of human normality, or should it use those moneys to improve provision for many more children of normal intelligence?

The fundamental demand by and behalf of the cognitively disabled for equality of recognition as human beings can be seen to generate a paradoxical demand for inequality. To allow the disabled some share in human flourishing they must be given a share of the social wealth which is out of all proportion to their numbers and which is greater than that allotted to many others.

To answer the above questions involves advancing a general conception of justice. Different conceptions of justice provide different answers to the question of what is owing in social provision to the cognitively disabled. For example, on a utilitarian conception justice is subservient to utility. Veatch's resource allocation dilemma will be dealt with by a simple method. It will be very unlikely that a pattern of allocation which allows improvements, perhaps marginal, in the happiness or preference satisfaction of the few, as opposed to utility gains for the majority, will be deemed just.

Fortunately for me, I have no space in this study to defend a developed theory of justice against its philosophical rivals. What I can do is outline the conception of justice which I think gives the best answer to the questions posed in this section and explain its consequences. The conception of justice I advance is congruent with the language and assumptions about the worth of persons employed in earlier stages of my argument. It is ultimately derived from Aristotle, though it has been developed and defended by a number of recent writers.[40] At the heart of this conception of justice are two things: an account of the human good and a principle of proportion or distribution concerning the way in which this good is shared among members of the community. It can therefore be styled a teleological conception of justice. In the teleological tradition, it is assumed that humanity shares a common nature (or species-being). This leads to the thought that there is a distinctively human good. The human good is perfectly, fully present in a human life which manifests all the virtues, or excellences of character and intellect. One who enjoys the good flourishes as a human being. Leaving aside visions of the perfected life, the teleological conception will claim that there is a list of basic goods which all must have if they are to have a chance of flourishing, an opportunity to embark on pursuit of the full good of a human existence. This list of basic goods generates a conception of social justice. A community is just when it recognises and embodies the principle of distribution mandating that all its members, so far as is practically possible, share in the basic human goods and thus have some real opportunity to flourish as human beings. The principle of distribution for the primary goods is thus equality: all should have them if means allow. Thereafter, the teleological theorist can accept that goods beyond the basic ones can be distributed in proportion to other things than mere humanity, mere possession of human species-being. People gain entitlements to the primary goods just in being human; they gain entitlements to goods beyond the primary goods by way of their talents and efforts, by way of patterns of inheritance and so on. A society owes all members of the human community, all who partake of human species-being, the basic human goods.

The differences between this conception of justice and its rivals, insofar as they bear on the problems of the cognitively disabled, can now be noted.

If justice is a simple function of utility, then we can justly refuse to give the basic goods to some provided that utility for a sufficient number of others is maximised (unless the utility generated by satisfying the basic goods is out of all proportion to satisfying other preferences). Not so on the teleological account: there are primary goods which all must have. The good of the community, so far as justice is concerned, is not maximum utility, but the common good, where this means the mutual sharing in the basic goods and thus the opportunity for human flourishing. People can be excluded from that common good through actions of their own (for example, criminals), but none are to be excluded simply on the grounds that to do so would increase the happiness or preference satisfaction of others.

The teleological conception repudiates the message of Nozick's *Anarchy, State and Utopia*, whereby giving appropriate care and education to the cognitively disabled could only be an act of charity on the part of the rest of the community. Nozick's leading thought is that justice must honour the inalienable right of each individual to his/her moral space. To tax individuals in order to secure or increase the well-being of others is to violate that space and treat those individuals as means to others' ends. But the teleological conception will reject the fundamental premise that justice, or ethics in general, is grounded upon rights. The existence and character of rights is rather subject to a prior consideration of what is morally right and wrong. No one has a right to do or possess something if that doing and possessing is morally wrong.[41] It is wrong to live in opulent splendour while others around one lack the means of subsistence or of developing minimally as human beings, so no citizen's rights are violated by having opulence taxed to give others the basics of the human good. There is no separate problem here about justifying the use of state power forcibly to take the entitlements of some in order to benefit others. If the others lack the primary goods, they are entitled to provision from the community. Members of the community are under an obligation to contribute to that provision and so are not entitled to withhold their aid; forcible taxation is but the practical, social working out of that obligation.[42]

The teleological conception cannot endorse the defence of strict egalitarianism in Veatch's *The Foundations of Justice*. Veatch contends that the just community will be one which enforces an equality in outcomes and holding between its members (though as his argument advances he waters this down to a strong idea of equality of opportunity). In the competition for resources, people should not be disadvantaged by 'extraneous factors' such as differences between their talents and endowments and the talents and endowments of others, differences which are merely the result of nature's lottery. The just community will be constantly striving to eliminate these handicapping differences and make the outcome of the competition as equal as possible. This entails, for Veatch, that those whose physical and mental endowments are very much below the average are to get massive compensation in material resources in the endeavour to bring their lifetime outcomes up to the level of those with a normal initial endowment. The message for society's obligations to invest in education and developmental training for the cognitively disabled is clear.[43]

Veatch's main argument for this radical egalitarianism is avowedly religious, indeed Biblical. Its true character thus needs to be addressed in Chapter 6 which follows. Leaving aside that religious basis, the teleological conception is likely to see little merit in the claim that justice in the community equates with doing the maximum possible to ensure equality in lifetime outcomes among its members. Equality cannot be a sufficient condition for justice apart from some conception of the human good. It would, after all, be possible to secure equality in outcome for all by seeing to it that all lived in poverty and neglect. Such an outcome would not be a realisation of the common good. Equality is not a necessary condition for justice insofar as inequalities in outcomes can perfectly well exist among members of a community while all share in the basic goods. On pragmatic grounds, there is much to be said for allowing the efforts and talents of individuals to give them valid claims for material rewards and for social goods such as honour and fame. For in that way individual effort will be encouraged and the totality of wealth and achievement in society will increase. Nozick is right to point to the ethically unacceptable consequences of frequent and radical redistributions of resources and goods to maintain a strict equality. Such policies do seem to deny the separateness of persons and ignore the side-constraints upon action which the separateness of persons invoke. Simply put: a drive to equality of outcome of the kind Veatch advocates will involve too many and too deep infractions of the freedom of individuals.[44] Moreover, the teleologist will contend (see below) that part of the human good includes self-development and the display and enjoyment of rational action. These primary goods are assaulted if people are not allowed a personal space around them or not allowed to gain entitlements to goods (material and otherwise) through their own efforts and talents.

The above comments carry over into reasons for rejecting Rawls' *A Theory of Justice*. Rawls, like Veatch, regards the talents and efforts of people as entailing little about their deserts and entitlements. Those talents are more properly part of the social pool, to be allowed to create advantages for individuals only to the extent that the worst off in society benefit.[45] This can likewise be seen from the teleological conception as embodying too thin a conception of the human good. Further reasons for rejecting Rawls' ideas as an appropriate theoretical structure for thinking about justice for the cognitively disabled stem from the fact that he sees principles of justice as the outcome of a hypothetical bargain between free and rational agents who are forced to judge impartially. We have noted in earlier chapters how this conception seems to exclude the cognitively disabled (or at least some of them) from the scope of justice altogether. One of Rawls' leading principles for the just society is the so-called 'maxi-min' rule: the rational contractors will agree as just those social arrangements which will maximise the position of the least worst off. It is not clear that such a rule applies to or helps the cognitively disabled. Rawls' emphasis on distribution of material goods in a just community suggests he means by 'worst off' the poor. While the cognitively disabled are surely going to be in that group, it is not evident that Rawls' principles give them a special place within it. The initial terms of the contract which generates justice seem to exclude the rational contractors worrying that they may suffer the misfortune of turning out to be cognitively disabled on the other side of the veil of ignorance. This appears to rule out them agreeing social arrangements which will provide an insurance policy mitigating the effects of that outcome. Recall: the initial terms of the contract are designed to create a social order in which individuals capable of pursuing a rational plan of life can do so in optimum conditions. As we have noted in earlier chapters, a contractarian conception of justice and right has problems about including in its scope those who do not possess a sense of justice, who lack rationality and autonomy.[46] Above all, the teleological conception is not compatible with the notion that justice is determined by working through what might be agreed on by imagined contractors, albeit in conditions of strict rationality and impartiality. Right-thinking individuals will agree on what is morally correct and socially just because it is right; but what is right is not decided by imagining how a bargaining session would go.

The teleological conception allows two kinds of entitlements to goods and holdings: needs and desert.[47] Needs correspond to the basic human goods and what is required for human beings to enjoy those; deserts are connected with the entitlements people earn through their efforts and relationships with others. Needs are primary insofar as all who are capable of having some share in human flourishing have the same foundation for needs and insofar as individuals' deserts cannot entitle them to hold on to goods if social use of them is required to satisfy others' needs for the basic goods. It follows from this, as noted above, that action to give another one or more of the basic goods falls under the requirements of justice and not merely benevolence. If society fails to satisfy some of its members' needs, in this technical sense of 'need', where it has the means to do so, then it is unjust. Justice and its demands, as these relate to needs and the basics of the human good, give expression to the notion of the moral equality of human beings as we have derived this from Simone Weil. To be recognised as human is for us to have our opportunity to partake in human flourishing respected. Meeting our need for the basic human goods is the concrete way in which this recognition and respect can be manifested. (Being accepted as individuals whose efforts can earn them entitlements to further goods beyond the primary ones is, of course, another manifestation of this equality.)

The nature of human flourishing and thus the basic goods is to be judged by reference to the species-being of humanity. Though there are concretely many and various ways in which human beings live and flourish, there is a common form to such living and flourishing which philosophical anthropology can discern through reflection on the distinctive powers, capacities and mode of being of the species. Human beings are embodied, organic beings in the first instance. A basic human good must therefore be life and physical health. Furthermore, human beings are creatures who reason, plan and are self-conscious. So the capacity for development as a reasoning, planning and self-conscious creature must be a good and what is necessary for this development is a human need. These modes of being are only possible given membership of communities. Social relations are also the constitutive means of other basic goods, such as pleasure. Opportunities for social relationships are thus one of the basic human goods. We could go on developing this account of the basic human goods. But the general message is clear enough. Lists of basic, primary human goods by contemporary thinkers in the teleological tradition vary – it is no part of teleological ethics to deny that accounts of the full character of human flourishing will not be affected by different world-views and ways of interpreting human experience.[48] Some of these variations amount to different ways of dividing up the same cake (for example, do we list social relationships as a separate good or include them as a component part of the good of rational, autonomous existence?). Despite these variations we can find agreement on a common core of goods, an agreement which is usefully pointed to in Brown's fourfold division of the primary human goods: the means of subsistence; pleasure; work, rest and play; and social relationships.[49]

Any account of human flourishing and any such list of basic human goods has obvious implications for our thought about the cognitively disabled. They are objects of justice by virtue of the facts that they share in human species-being (albeit, they show that species-being in an impaired manner) and are born into the human community. By the very fact of suffering impairments in the typical cognitive make-up of the human being, their ability to enjoy an existence manifesting the basic goods is threatened. It follows from this that they are by definition individuals who are at some risk of being barred from any participation in human flourishing via the basic goods. It also follows that, if it is possible through appropriate care, education and therapy for them to partake of these primary goods, then they have needs in the technical sense employed here: that is, entitlements, claims upon others which must in justice be met. This entails that the past incarceration of these people in institutions where little but their bodily needs were met, and with the intention of ensuring that they were kept out of the way of society at large, was not merely a failure in compassion but also an offence against justice.

Let us return to Veatch's example of the cognitively disabled child who needs a heavy investment of financial and personal resources to help it enjoy the rudiments of a developed existence as a thinking, communicative and social being. Our account surely establishes an entitlement in justice to those resources on behalf of that child. This entitlement should give that child a stronger claim in justice against the communal wealth than that generated by the benefits in further intellectual advancement for normal children if the money were spent on them. This is an example of the way in which the teleological conception of justice is similar in one respect to Rawls' conception: it mandates a focus on the least advantaged in the community. It creates a social obligation to ensure that all who can share in the common good are given an opportunity so to share.

We must concede at the close of this discussion of justice that the teleological conception outlined does not, as presented, deal with the myriad questions of detail which the claims of justice for the cognitively disabled raise. What has been offered has been broad-brush and theoretical. No detailed prescription for resource allocation follows from it. For example, the discussion of the case from Veatch does not tell us exactly where to draw the line in educational provision for a child with significant cognitive disability. In drawing such a line considerations of utility must be relevant. For after material and human resources have been allocated to giving such a child the rudiments of speech and other basic skills, the question will have to be addressed of how much more is to be allocated given that further allocations may generate little further progress in development, whereas those resources would have a greater utility if devoted elsewhere. I have no formula to hand for answering such questions of detail.

6
Theological and Religious Issues

The relevance of theology

We have seen that many contemporary moral philosophers regard our moral judgements as standing in need of justification. These judgements need to be anchored on foundations provided by philosophy. Many of our practices reflect the belief that all human beings enjoy a special status and share a fundamental moral equality. This belief needs to be grounded. We need to find some property (or set of properties), over and above being human, the possession of which explains why human beings share this special status. The principle that beings with this property have this status is more fundamental than the assertion that all human beings alike have intrinsic worth just in being human beings. A principle such as 'all creatures who are autonomous and rational are intrinsically valuable' is thus more certain than any pre-philosophical claim about the worth of human beings. Moreover, philosophical reflection can show by argument why the property referred to in any such principle is worthy of being part of the moral foundations. So, philosophy can answer the further question as to why a property such as self-consciousness is uniquely valuable. Utilitarian and contractarian theories of the good and the right illustrate this endeavour.

The shape of utilitarian, contractarian and other contemporary moral philosophies is influenced by empiricism. That is to say, the enterprise of seeking foundations to ethics assumes that the properties which ground ordinary affirmations of moral value must be empirically discernible. This metaphysical commitment is in turn deduced from an epistemological requirement: only empirical properties are capable of grounding public, rational discussion of moral values. The predilection for empirical grounds of value can also be seen to reflect a form of scientism. It is assumed that the theories and vocabulary of natural science are sufficient to describe all that is real in the world. Hence the basis of value can only be empirical properties of people and objects and the attitudes they invoke in human beings.

We noted in Chapter 1 that these empiricist, secular accounts of value confront a test-case in the instance of the cognitively disabled. For any set of empirical properties which is the putative ground of the worth of human beings is always likely to be present in only some human beings. The response of secular proponents of bioethics is the heroic one of not letting customary moral perceptions get in the way of a good theory: they deny the severely cognitively disabled, along with other types of human being, the status of persons and thus the special worth possessed by the rest of us.

Defenders of theologically-based ways of writing about the worth of human life will see in the implications of secular approaches to the worth of human beings a *reductio* of the attempt to ground that worth on empirical qualities. They will press the following dilemma: either we accept a theological (or religious or revealed) basis for the ascription of fundamental worth to all human beings, or we discriminate among human beings, denying personhood to very many of them. The claim of theological ethics is that secularism leads to something decent people must regard as horrendous. Reflection on the moral status of the mentally handicapped provides a moral argument for the truth of some brand of religious metaphysics.

In the remainder of this chapter we shall follow the theological attempt to use the mentally handicapped to refute a purely secular ethics. We need to note now that, for all that such approaches depart from the substantive conclusions about human beings favoured by secular bioethics, they agree in the grounding principle that ethical perceptions need a foundation in metaphysics, that is in a theory of human nature and value.

Grounding moral worth on relationship to God

Basil Mitchell is one who has argued that those who wish to assert the traditional claim that all human beings have intrinsic worth, and are to be protected against harm and exploitation accordingly, will be intellectually embarrassed in that assertion unless they embrace a theistic metaphysics. He notes that 'our intense feeling for the value of the individual personality has not developed to the same extent in other traditions'.[1] Nor is this surprising, he continues. Within the Christian tradition an account can be given of why the individual human being is worthy of moral respect. That tradition offers a metaphysical anthropology whereby every human being, regardless of personal qualities and social standing, enjoys a unique relation to God. Every human being has an eternal destiny in virtue of this relationship. God offers salvation to every human being as such. He notes that on the traditional theological view every human being is an object of unconditional worth. We are not loved by God because of qualities or merits we possess, for any such ground of divine love would make that love conditional. If it were conditional then it would decline to the extent that we lost these qualities or merits and might cease altogether. By contrast, only an unconditional worth and unconditional love can be universal. None of us deserve unconditional love more than any others. Many secular writers wish to retain a sense of the unconditionality and universality of human worth. One way they have tried to do so is illustrated by Kant. We see in Kant's ethical writings, according to Mitchell, an endeavour to replace Christian language of the universal divine–human relation with talk of the dignity of each and every human being as a rational creature, possessed of an awareness of the moral law and the ability thereby to pursue happiness via virtue. Our relationship to the moral law and our moral destiny stands in place of the religious picture of our relation to God and our future life with God. According to Mitchell, there are two problems with the Kantian reconstruction of the theological picture. First, Mitchell notes that its emphasis on the universal possession of reason gives a picture of human nature which is too dualistic and intellectualised.[2] Second, we observe that the possession of practical reason as Kant defines that is not an invariant and universal property of the species and will not therefore support a belief in the unconditional and universal sanctity of human life.

The above line of argument gives rise to what Mitchell styles 'the dilemma of the traditional conscience'. This is the dilemma formed from the joint desires to hold on to a traditional belief in the sanctity of human life while getting rid of the religious foundation of that belief. The two desires cannot, consistently, be held together. The consistent secularists are those who do not try to maintain the dignity of each and every human life. Mitchell gives his case focus by taking up the Christian claim that each and every human being is to be loved for his or her own sake. He notes that many have found this an odd claim to make. Outside Christianity, or theistic religion, it has seemed more natural to hold that people are to be loved for their individuating merits or deserts. He quotes Freud to the effect that if I love someone he or she must be *worthy* of that love, either because of intrinsic merits or because of some close relationship to me. By contrast, the Christian injunction to love all human beings has a foundation not in the distinguishing merits of individuals but in the fact that all human beings are beloved by God. That fact goes along with others: they are redeemed by God's saving work, bear the image of God and so forth.[3] We are under a divine injunction to love all our neighbours as ourselves and this injunction rests on the fact that all are the objects of a divine regard, which in turn is definitive of the human condition.

The 'dilemma of the traditional conscience' is intended to be part of a case which leads from the recognition of key features of morality to the embrace of a religious metaphysics. The key problem with the case Mitchell presents is that it faces its own dilemma, a dilemma which threatens to rob it of any force. This can be seen when we ask the following question: is there anything in human beings which makes them fit objects of divine love? If the defender of the necessity of a theological basis to the moral equality of human beings answers 'No' to this question, then the divine love appears wholly arbitrary. If the theological moralist answers 'Yes', then we are back to the position of secular ethics – we must find some characteristic which all human beings possess which marks them out as worthy of special respect.

Mitchell feels the pressure of this dilemma. He contends that the universal divine love for creatures cannot merely be 'an external relation which could be added to or withdrawn from the human situation, leaving everything else unchanged'. It is, rather, part and parcel of our having been made in a certain way by God, namely as creatures capable of relationship with him. Being made in this way means having 'capacities for development and response' and being 'free agents, capable of choosing between good and evil, responding to or rejecting love . . .'.[4] These traits make human beings appropriate objects of divine love. Mitchell is honest enough to acknowledge that this conception of divine love having an appropriate object reintroduces the problem of how all human beings can be seen as having a special dignity. Mitchell has in effect reintroduced the notion that freedom and the capacity for moral choice are important in giving all human beings an equal, unconditional worth. He has done so because freedom and the capacity for moral choice are the foundations of distinctively personal relationships. Human beings are constituted for eternal life: 'a loving communion with God and with other men, which may begin on earth but can be fulfilled only in heaven'.[5] Genuine communion of this kind must,

Mitchell implicitly argues, depend on our being capable of self-consciously 'responding to or rejecting love'. This, then, must be a mode of responding to love which is different in kind from, say, the way in which a pet dog or cat might respond to the love of its owner. The relational destiny for human beings depends on special relational capacities, which in turn depend on something very much like the secular favourite: autonomous agency. So, as Mitchell notes, problems still arise (they are the same old problems) 'as to where the limits of humanity are to be drawn'. The theologian's response is: 'Here we can only rely on the conviction that what there is to be saved God will save and, where there is doubt, [we must] treat with respect all who share the human form'.[6]

Mitchell has concluded that there must be something within human beings which makes them fit objects of a distinctive kind of divine love, otherwise that love becomes something merely external and arbitrary. The trait which makes human beings a fit object for divine regard is their capacity for full interpersonal relationships. That trait in turn depends on others which take us back to the distinguishing features of truly personal agency. Since it is just the attenuation and absence of those features which we use to mark out a rough class of cognitively disabled people, we are back with the familiar problem: that in which the cognitively disabled are different from the rest of humanity is that which some moral theories say makes them of lower moral standing. Mitchell's theological approach to the question of the grounds of moral worth and dignity encourages a discriminatory mode of valuing after all. It takes our attention, albeit indirectly, toward features which set the cognitively disabled apart from the rest of humanity. By contrast, if we focus, as I have argued in Chapter 3 we must, on the fact that the disabled are afflicted human beings, then we perceive them as morally at one with us.[7] Seen in this light, the theological metaphysics which Mitchell thinks must come to the aid of our moral perceptions turns out to be a way of distracting us from those perceptions.

It would be unfair to conclude that the problems encountered in Mitchell mean that his theological metaphysics offers no advance on the treatment of moral regard found in contemporary bioethics. For example, given that the picture of all human beings as fit for communion with God introduces a key teleological conception of human life, then it also avoids the occasionalism we found in secular moral theory. There is no temptation on Mitchell's account to divide a human life into stages and mark out some of these stages as worthy of moral respect and others as not. What our dilemma does show is that, when it comes to the foundations of the moral equality of human beings, Mitchell's route of finding a correlate for divine love in the human endowment does not show reliance on the moral perceptions and reactions surrounding mere humanity to be unreliable. This particular way of applying theology to the problem has to go via the possession of traits on the part of human beings, traits which are discriminatory. How do things fare if we take the other horn of the dilemma? Perhaps divine love has no correlate in human nature which makes it deserved or appropriate. Perhaps this love, in and of itself, bestows a unique worth, and since this love embraces all humanity it can be the proper ground of moral equality.

The view that divine regard is the necessary and sufficient condition of the worth of all human beings is argued for by David Pailin. His conclusion is that 'Like every other person . . . [the mentally handicapped individual] has ultimate worth because, and only because, God values him'.[8] This conclusion is reached via the leading principle that the value of things is the value they have for sentient creatures. What makes something of worth is that someone or other cherishes that thing. Except for God himself – who is the ultimate source of value rather than one thing amongst the things which have value – the basis of worth is the fact that someone wants or needs or regards something: 'Worth is something that is bestowed by being loved, being wanted, and being cherished'.[9] Pailin appears to have two arguments for this general account of worth. One is based on the fact that many things in ordinary life which are deemed to be of value are so only because they are the object of some human being's regard and not because they are intrinsically better than other things (think of your favourite photograph). The other argument is based on the falsity of the main alternative to the relational view of worth considered, namely the thesis that things have worth in terms of their contribution to human society or advancement or whatever. Any contributory view of human worth will in particular be flawed because it will quickly turn out to lead to the devaluation of those who are not fit, healthy and able. Contributory bases of worth will be discriminatory in an unacceptable way.

Pailin's first argument from the premise that many things have worth only because of their relation to some human being's regard is weak. We can accept that, in suitable circumstances, the regard of some human being is a sufficient condition for an object having worth. But that does not entail that being the object of someone's regard is a necessary condition for having worth. There is thus no need to oppose the 'insight that value is fundamentally something that is given' to the position that value is 'inherent in an object'.[10] The value of some things can be established via the first route and of other things by the second route. Some objects may be established as valuable by a combination of both routes. It is true that human beings will not feel themselves to be beings of value if they are not valued by others – a point about the basis of self-respect noted in earlier chapters of this study. But that does not entail that the devalued person is worthless, as Pailin's thesis might at first sight imply. We must distinguish the sense of worth from worth itself. Only thus can we lament the fact that some people are devalued by all around them and though they have worth enjoy no sense of having it.

To claim that some things or some people have no value save insofar as someone else values them raises paradoxes. It rules out the possibility that some things are the object of regard because they are seen to be of value, and so threatens to make the direction of regard arbitrary. Further, it implies that the neglected, forgotten human being is automatically of no value. This last paradox is felt by Pailin and met by bringing in God. Since God values each and every human being, the fact that some human beings are devalued or ignored by their fellows counts for nothing. Divine love establishes an equality of worth amongst us all, for its universality entails that there never is a person who is not the object of a loving, cherishing regard.[11]

Pailin's account of the worth of human beings appears to have theoretical advantages. It secures the moral equality of all of us while employing a minimal ontology of value. Things are the objects of pro-attitudes on the part of sentient creatures. The postulation of God's love for us all gives us all value without having to bring anything else in. However, the paradoxes in the position can be deepened to the point of making it implausible. We can note straightway that it is impossible in terms of this simple position to explain why God selects human beings to be the object of loving regard. Mitchell's view has an answer to this query. Human beings have intrinsic traits which make them fit for personal relationships, relationships involving choice, freedom and moral agency. The divine altruism or other-directedness then serves to make the beings who have these traits objects of divine love. But of course this view has problems with moral equality. If, by contrast, the divine regard is literally based on nothing in its objects, if there is nothing which evokes it, it is hard to see why God has it for all human beings. God would not be acting wrongly if he made only some of us objects of love. Furthermore, it is hard to see why human beings *especially* should be the objects of love. If there is nothing in humanity as such which makes it worthy of this divine love, then there is no reason we can offer why earthworms or rocks should not be objects of an equal love and therefore have an equal endowed worth.

Independently of Pailin's views about value, it is hard to see from a theological perspective why God's love and special regard should track the boundaries of the human species. If it tracks qualities such as the capacity for personal agency, it won't track the species boundary. If God's love does not track qualities, such as autonomy, it is hard to see how it might settle on any one kind of thing in creation rather than another. Explaining how we human beings should have a special regard for all human beings is easier. In our case, we can say of the disabled, afflicted person 'there goes a fellow human being' with all that implies about our sharing a common life and lot with that person. Such perception will go hand in hand with the capacity to react with pity and compassion to the afflicted. That, we have argued in Chapter 3, provides a sufficient condition for regarding human beings as having a special value. We might bring in thoughts about the Incarnation to give room for the divine perception of 'a common lot' in the theological perspective. But apart from the complexities and strains on our understanding introduced by that notion, we would face the further problem of why we should think that the story of the Incarnation shows God identifying with humanity as such, rather than, again, with that portion capable of personal relations, autonomy or the like.

A final, serious problem with Pailin's invocation of the universality of divine love is this: on his view of value there should be no need to bring in a universal divine love to explain how all human beings are worthy of the same fundamental respect. That there are neglected, forgotten wretches whom no human agent cares for should not raise the question for Pailin of how we can establish their worth as persons. If value is bestowed by the regard of others, then these folk have no value. If we feel that they must have value, the same value as people we know and cherish, then that feeling is shown by the Pailin theory to be illusory. They are not a problem for the theory. The theory of value gives a verdict on the value of neglected, forgotten people and that verdict should be accepted, if the theory is sound. The need to invoke divine agency can only be felt with any urgency because it is accepted that human beings are valuable as such, regardless of how others may regard them. But that is a perception which is fundamentally alien to the theory. Our having that perception and our taking it seriously shows we do not accept the view of value which creates the alleged problem.

Let us review the case for rejecting the notion that drafting in theology can help us with the fundamental problem of how to defend the moral standing of the cognitively disabled.

To defend the moral standing of these disabled people we must defend the moral equality of all human beings against those theories which tell us that standing is based on the possession of qualities of cognition and agency; any such approach will be discriminatory and mark the cognitively disabled as an out-group. In Chapter 3, two complementary ideas were the basis of a defence of the perception of the moral equality of all human beings. One was possession by all of us of a distinctive human species-being or nature. It was a sufficient condition for giving others moral standing that we saw them as possessing this species-being or shared nature, no matter how impaired or undeveloped it was in them. The second idea was that we could see all human beings as possessing with us a common human life or lot. This perception is operative and alive in pity and compassion and correspondingly dormant in acts of oppression and cruelty. Both ideas support a humanistic outlook by way of nurturing a sense of human solidarity. Both prevent a binary mode of valuing human beings in which the properties of some selected 'us' become necessary conditions of standing and thereby inevitably define a 'them' who lack these properties. Both ideas, but particularly the second, arise out of moral response itself (so that, for example, it makes sense to say that the other, afflicted human being is *revealed* as at one with me through my compassionate response to his or her needs).

If it is right to see a sense of human solidarity as sufficient to affirm the moral equality of the cognitively disabled in the face of threats from bioethics, then it is indeed hard to see how bringing divine evaluations into the picture is necessary.

To this point, the reply to the argument that we need theology to ground our perceptions of the moral equality of human beings has been defensive: there is no reason, on reflection, to think that the considerations outlined in Chapter 3 need to be supplemented by theological perspectives in order to make those considerations strong enough to rebut discriminatory accounts of human worth. In particular, considerations reminiscent of the Euthyphro dilemma indicate that the argument 'All human beings are of value because God values/loves them' needs to be supplemented by some of the very points made in Chapter 3. From this conclusion, reflection on the contribution of theology to a defence of the moral equality of human beings may go in two ways. It may be argued that theology is positively harmful to this defence, or it may be conceded that it can add to the defence, albeit it is not necessary.

We may reject the appeal to God on the following grounds: calling upon the divine in the hands of a Mitchell or a Pailin is essentially calling upon a metaphysical perspective in aid of our human perceptions and practices, and that means endeavouring to occupy ground external to those perceptions and practices, from which they can in turn be justified. This, then, looks like another attempt to see justification of our sense of the moral equality of human beings by a putative use of a transcendent reason. Endeavours to justify our moral perceptions from within a metaphysical perspective will inevitably undermine the immanent means we have of grounding those perceptions.

On the other hand, we may accept that theology and religion have a legitimate role to play in bolstering moral equality. Thus it could be argued that, once we grant that human beings typically have a minimal level of personal capacities which make them open to a relationship with God and fit objects of loving regard by God, then the fact that they are loved by God may increase our sense of their worth. That sense will be further strengthened by the thought that the relationship they have with God will give them an eternal destiny which they may enjoy regardless of how they fare in this life. The problem that some human beings may be so disabled as to lack the minimal capacities for enjoying a relationship with God can be set aside if we grant that God, in the manner indicated in Chapter 3, regards and values human individuals as members of a kind and thus cherishes them all regardless of attainments. Then God's love will see to it that those so disabled will be able to partake of some form of the eternal relationship with God offered to all, perhaps by being transformed after death. So, by these means, we could after all argue that the divine love and regard could track the boundary of the human species.

I offer no adjudication on how the debate outlined above may go. However, in the next section I do note that traditional accounts of human–divine relationships in at least the Christian tradition are heavily intellectualised and give great weight to human beings as moral agents in a moral drama. They thus tend of their nature to be exclusive of cognitively disabled people.

This part of the discussion can be brought to a close with a simple point. If we accept the conclusion that theology is not necessary to justify our sense of the moral equality of all human beings, then we may feel that, after all, this is a good thing. For if it were essential to employ theological premises and perspectives to preserve this sense of solidarity, it would not be available to the many who cannot accept theological claims. From a moral point of view, it would be bad if humane practices and outlooks do depend on theological beliefs. The world is full of thinkers who will be only too happy to abandon the demands of humanism if they do depend essentially on religious grounds: witness the likes of Kuhse, Rachels and Singer.

The cognitively disabled as a theological problem

The aim of this section is to explore ways in which the existence and character of cognitive disability provides a positive challenge to the plausibility of theological outlooks. Soteriology and evil will be its chief themes.

A religion like Christianity places human life in a soteriological context. What this means for the theologian is spelled out by Kevin Vanhoozer thus: 'The human being is a "metaphysical animal", constituted by a desire for what is greater than itself, for ultimate reality'.[12] To see the human being as a metaphysical animal is to see human life as teleological. The human being is constituted for an end which is more than natural. It is an end which involves relationship with a transcendent creator. We bear the image of God insofar as we have the basic set of capacities which makes us capable of fulfilling that end and gaining right relationship with God. Theologies differ over the account they give of the exact nature of that relationship and thus of the precise set of human capacities which constitute the image of God in the human being. Christian theologies also differ over the question of what exactly has gone wrong with the human condition such that it prevents the realisation of our relation to God and necessitates the redemptive work of God through Christ. One thing that runs through these many detailed and competing variations on the salvation theme in Christian theology is that both the teleology within human nature and the ills which prevent its realisation have a strong moral character. The capacities which constitute the image of God in us, the disorder in human nature and life preventing these from being truly realised, and the final goal for which we are saved are all facets of a being who is moral.

A schematic way of bringing out this moral dimension is found in Hick's distinction between ego and self.[13] Human beings exist naturally as egos. That is, they are centres of will and experience. They claim actions and experiences as their own. But they are also selves insofar as they do not flourish apart from relationships with others. As moral beings, as selves, they can rise above the concerns and perspectives of the ego and share a life with others. The teleology of salvation is that of a direction toward an existence of pure selfhood in which ego concern is left behind. This is a journey in moral development. Because many religions unite in seeing the perfection of selfhood as involving not just living in ego-transcending relationship to others, but in relationship to some ultimate, non-mundane reality, so they regard the final realisation of self as involving some form of union with the divine. Within Christian dogmatics, ego-centredness is sealed by sin and can only be defeated by the saving work of Christ. Any journey away from ego-life to true selfhood involves sharing in a grace mediated by Christ and some kind of imitation of his own ego-free existence, his own model of being and living for others. In this way human destiny is relational, but not finally anthropocentric, rather it is theocentric.[14] However the causes of ego-centredness are described, however the nature of the freedom from its grip wrought by Christ is envisaged, we have a picture of human life set in the context of a moral drama and directed toward a moral goal achieved by exercise of facets of the moral personality.

The problem with this general picture, and its many individual variants in theological thought, is that it tends of its very nature to exclude the cognitively disabled. The degree to which they are cognitively disabled will be the degree to which they are left out of the general picture and have no place in the metaphysical teleology in which human life is set. We can indicate the problem by going back to Hick's ego/selfhood distinction. If religion tells us that human life involves a transformation from ego-life to a life of self, then what about those individuals who, through mental impairment, never develop a full, or even a minimal, ego-life? To exist as an ego is to exist as a source of self-conscious experience and agency. It is to be able to refer experiences to an 'I' conceived as existing through time and as having its own point of view on the world. It is to be able to act with a sense of one's own interests as against a sense of the interests of others. It is to be capable of pursuing those interests over time and in opposition or indifference to the interests of others. It is to be a rational and planning agent. What this means, of course, is that to be an ego is to have just those capacities for reflection, understanding and agency whose absence in some significant degree marks someone out as cognitively disabled. It is thus that the cognitively disabled are excluded from the moral drama that is salvation.

Some Christian accounts of the image of God and the human being as 'metaphysical animal' are rationalistic in an explicit way. This is so for Thomas Aquinas' account of the human journey toward love of and union with God.[15] According to Aquinas the human being is designed to grow to perfection. Human perfection consists in a perfected life in God, but it is also grounded in our lives as free and rational creatures. As free and rational creatures we are capable of conceiving of, and pursuing, happiness and the good. We are creatures gifted with intellect and will. This possession of a rational soul marks us out as different in kind from plants and animals. Intellect and will are disordered in the sinful human being. In a variety of ways, God through Christ offers means by which this disorder can be overcome and the human being be set again on a path toward perfect union with God. The achievement of that union will involve the perfection of life in the moral and the theological virtues (faith, hope and charity). But it will crucially involve in addition the perfection of intellect and will in the transformed human being. Human volition will be perfected via a process of evermore effective pursuit of the good. Intellect will grow more perfect in its grasp of what the good consists in and in the final blessed state of the vision of God, this eternal vision being the realisation of complete blessedness. In these ways blessedness in the form of the vision of God cannot simply be *given* to the saved human being. Inculcation of a range of intellectual, moral and theological virtues is necessary in order for the individual to acquire the ability to partake in that vision. So the path to blessedness is closed to those incapable of the necessary development.

It must follow from an account of human teleology such as Aquinas provides that, to the extent that human beings are defective in the foundation of moral capacities, namely intellect and will, then they are incapable of blessedness. They will be excluded from perfect relationship with God and thus salvation. So Aquinas' account is written as if there are no cognitively disabled people, or as if they do not matter. This blindness cannot be put down to the deficiencies of a thirteenth-century outlook. We have seen above that it is central in any Christian account of salvation to employ moral categories in order to conceive of what human beings are saved from and what they are saved for. One reason for this is that without an emphasis on moral potentiality there is no room to place a barrier of human *sin* between human and divine and therefore no need for a divinely granted means of attaining salvation.

The exclusion of the cognitively disabled can also be seen in the account of Vanhoozer, which we have referred to already and which seems superficially at least to be so different from that of Aquinas. The sequence 'ego–life–selfhood' is present in a fashion in Vanhoozer. He characterises human existence as relational. The fulfilment of that life is thus seen when human beings exist in perfect relationship with their natural environment, their fellow human beings and with God.[16] By 'relationship' Vanhoozer obviously has in mind relationships of the kind possible for cognitive agents, since he emphasises 'the self as communications centre'.[17] A person is a communicative agent in a web of communicative relationships with others. Vanhoozer places great stress on human beings as masters and inheritors of language. The root and apotheosis of sin is the attempt to assert one's autonomy over and against others and thus live without others and without God. This is a condition which Vanhoozer labels 'autism': 'that shrivelling of the self to the point of total self-absorption'.[18] The exclusionary character of this picture is obvious from the fact that the focus is on the human *failure* to exercise capacities of living in right relation to and for others through sinful preoccupation with the ego. The picture is painted without reference to those many human beings whose relationships to others are very limited and impaired not because of any failure on their part, but because they lack the cognitive endowments necessary to exist fully as communicative agents. The exclusion, and ignorance, of the cognitively disabled is sealed by the unfortunate use of 'autism' in Vanhoozer's rhetoric. As noted in Chapter 2, autistic individuals are not typically without the capacity to relate to others. They are not in that respect totally self-absorbed. Rather, their relationships and communications with others are impaired. More importantly what leads to the state Vanhoozer labels 'autism' is described by him as 'sinful autonomy'. What lead to real autism are neurological factors which have nothing to do with sin. Vanhoozer's sketch of the human condition simply has nothing to say about those many human beings who are impaired in their relations with others through no fault of their own but through their biology.

All soteriologies are formally similar. They will contain an account of something from which we are saved, something by which we are saved and some goal for which are saved. It is inevitable that the starting point, means and goal of salvation depend on viewing the human agent as rational and morally aware. Once religion abandons attempts to get the divine to sort out worldly ills (such as poor crops, our proneness to disease and the like), the problems in the human condition which it addresses will be moral and spiritual, that is problems which cannot be overcome through such things as better science and agriculture. There is no reason to scoff at such endeavours to see human life as a moral drama. We have seen, however, that they are necessarily exclusive of part of the human race: namely that portion which, through cognitive disability (or early death, or the effects of crippling poverty, or any number of factors) has not had the chance to develop as full moral agents. Such folk may not have an ego to the extent that they need to be, or are capable of being, helped to escape from the domination of ego-life in order to achieve the goal of a true selfhood rooted in right relation to the divine. Thus it might seem that the soteriological systems of the great religions, with their metaphysics of the human, have nothing to say to very many human creatures. Focusing on such people, we might be tempted to say that these soteriological systems are just irrelevant.

One may object to the above strictures that in many traditional religious communities, including Christian ones, the cognitively disabled have been regarded as divine gifts, indeed as blessed by God. They have played the role, also occupied by children, of examples of moral innocence – the very delay in their development of ego-life and selfhood has paradoxically enabled them to function in some contexts as exemplars of those who stand closest to God. I can confirm from my own experience that there is something wonderfully touching and attractive in the inability of an autistic teenager, like a toddler, to tell a lie in the full sense (to act with the design of inducing a false belief in another). Is this religious tendency simply incompatible with the accounts of the human drama described above? Is it the case that they point to a quite different way of conceptualising the human–divine relationship? I have no definitive, worked-out answers to these questions. There is, however, an obvious way of integrating this kind of regard for children and the childlike with the notion that true relation to God comes after the completion of a journey to selfhood. The child and the innocent disabled person manifestly represent in the concrete a negative component or aspect of the fully morally developed self: the inability to do or to choose evil. In the fully developed moral self this inability will be a function of a person's *second nature*. It will be acquired via a struggle in a life which has known, and still knows, what evil is and what it is to choose evil. In the young child or the cognitively disabled person the inability will be part of their *first nature* and reflect an inability to choose evil out of a lack of any conception of what evil may be. It is in this negative respect that we might, paradoxically, be bidden to strive after the innocence we find in those whose ego-development and selfhood is arrested.

It might be objected further that great world religions such as Christianity do offer visions of an entire world restored to wholeness in the eschaton. The Kingdom of God will be one in which the entire created order will be remade and restored. In it disease and handicap will be no more.[19] In reply to this objection, I can only say that I am at a loss to fathom what such restoration precisely consists in. Nor can I see any intelligible connection between human moral failings and an entire world being disordered and capable of producing disease and handicap. (Stories like those linking a broken world to God's punishment for Adam and Eve's sin are intelligible up to a point, but obviously fail of moral coherence when pressed.) It will be part of such visions of a world restored in God's Kingdom that the disabled will be transformed, will rise again, perfect and unimpaired. Such a vision may go along with conceiving of intermediate states of existence between this three score years and ten and the final eschaton. The disabled will not be fit to attain blessedness just in being reborn whole. They will gain a fully-fledged ego-life in being reborn, but they will need a further process of moral and spiritual development to acquire a selfhood. Just such a vision of successive stages of existence in which a divine teleology for all human being is gradually worked out is outlined in Hick's *Death and Eternal Life*. It is notable that Hick argues for this eschatology by reference to the very premise of the moral equality of all human beings operative in this study. Hick reasons from the 'Christian-humanist' premise of the ultimate value of each and every human person. Given that premise, we should regard the suffering (or disability) of any one of us as unjustified unless all of us are destined in the long run for ultimate bliss. Only the ultimate sharing of all of us in a perfected life can make the cosmic order just. To accept less is to acquiesce in devaluing some human beings. Concern for justice and the value of each and every one of us forms the basic religious argument for immortality.[20]

Much of this picture will strike the secular humanist as so much wishful thinking. The existence of incurable and incompensatable cognitive disability does mark one way in which the world we live in does not reflect the values we live by. But it is reasonable to use this fact as a premise in an argument for the conclusion that the world must therefore be, underneath and in the long run, one in which all human affliction disappears and is compensated, only if we have a prior belief that the world must be run in conformity with our deepest values. It manifestly is not, the secular humanist will argue. A further problem with the soteriological conception is the problem of identity. As David Pailin dryly points out:

> The post-mortem existence of handicapped persons is thus treated as something like recovery from an illness. Just as a person may get over

a bout of pneumonia and display again the physical and mental vigour which she or he had before the illness, so after death a person may be expected to be transformed into a state of personal being in which he or she is not handicapped.[21]

Pailin goes on to point to the obvious difficulty in this line of thought: a cognitive disability (such as Down's syndrome) is determinative of an individual's entire being. A sudden change, in particular, to being a person without a trace of such a disability throws into question the extent to which that person's identity has been conserved. This point is not meant to be a knock-down refutation of the idea of post-mortem transformation, merely an indication of an area of difficulty.

Hick's vision of the world as a teleological system designed to produce a final fulfilment for all is a facet of his solution to the problem of evil. The world contains the possibility of harm and affliction to human beings because of its teleological structure. It is designed so that it will serve as the background against which human beings may grow morally and spiritually. The harm and affliction that is cognitive disability is a by-product of this overarching purpose. In order to serve the moral and spiritual goal behind it, the world must exist as an independent sphere in which human agency can be exercised freely. That in turn entails that its integrity as a natural system acting according to its own laws must be respected by God. The upshot is that human beings must take their chances in a physical cosmos whose fundamental structures can both serve and harm human life. Divine providence is limited by itself in order to secure this measure of independence for the world. Being limited in this way, the possibility of damage to human beings cannot be ruled out.[22] The disabled are amongst the casualties of this teleology, but the entire scheme is redeemed by the good it makes possible.

A number of points need to be made about the way in which the cognitively disabled fit into the problem of evil. First, it surely is the case that cognitive disability as we have defined it is a contributor to the sum of natural evil in the world.[23] This follows from our assertion that to have a significant diminution of the species-typical powers of cognition is, to that extent, to be afflicted. It is linked to the thought that we would prevent the occurrence of cognitive disability if we had the means. Second, we should see and accept the force of Hick's contention, noted above, that the teleology of good and evil framing the world according to theism has to lead to the good of the individuals who are its present casualties. A teleological vision which leaves these human beings excluded from final, fulfilling good, but contends that the chance of salvation for the rest justifies affliction to the minority, will be open to the charge of moral corruption. Such a vision is based on a gross kind of cosmic expediency. Hence, it is with reason that Hick appeals to the necessity of those who are afflicted, those who suffer, being part of the 'eventual all-justifying fulfilment of the human potential in a perfected life'.[24] The afflicted have to be an integral part of the goal for which the creation has been designed. Third, reflection on the problem of evil throws doubt on the theological premise of Robert Veatch's argument (set out in Chapter 5 above) for interpreting justice for the cognitively disabled in terms of strict equality of outcome. That premise is that God desires equality of outcome for his human creatures. But if anything is apparent from a survey of the naturally caused evils in this world, it is that they are not distributed equally. There can be no inference from the world as we find it to the conclusion that its creator cares about equality. If we bring a belief that he does so care to the world from other sources (such as the Bible), the distribution of natural evil points to great problems in reconciling such a belief with the character of creation. Fourth, and finally, the problem of evil now can be seen to highlight the difficulty that the cognitively disabled present to a theistic soteriology. For the relevant teleological structure justifying God's ways is of a moral kind. The inevitability of natural evil is traded off against the fact that it is part of a system which makes moral and spiritual development possible for autonomous, free human agents. But it is precisely this telos from which the cognitively disabled are excluded. They can only be included if we indulge in Hick's postulation of a series of post-mortem lives in which modes of development and growth not possible for many in the here and now are opened up.

To say that the cognitively disabled are part of the sum of natural evil any theodicy must take account of is not of course to say that cognitively disabled people are evil or represent in themselves so many instances of negative value. As human individuals, they have worth and standing and are deserving of respect and compassionate concern. They have a stake in, and a claim upon, any just human community. They can enrich and reward the lives of those close to them. From a theistic perspective, we would not say that God does not love those who are so disabled. What is evil is that they are afflicted. The same, we noted in Chapter 4, could be said about the diabetic. That we would do all that we can to prevent the occurrence of diabetes in the future and rid the world of it, does not at all imply or entail that we think of diabetics as evil or as instances of negative value, or that God does not love and value them as God loves and values the healthy. Despite all that, we should prevent the occurrence of these afflictions by any licit means. If we adopt the anthropomorphism typical of theodicy's speculations, we can imagine an all-good and all-powerful God reasoning that the world-system should be arranged so that diabetes, Down's syndrome and autism never occur in it because these are afflictions. That God did not arrange matters thus legitimately provokes questioning.

If we cannot accept the lush religious ontology adumbrated in Hick's *Death and Eternal Life*, what kind of telos can we hold out for the cognitively disabled? Well, naturally, on a secular, humanist perspective it will be a modest one. It will consist in the hope for a just human community. In such a community, the cognitively disabled will be loved and respected as human beings. Their disabilities will be noted by the rest of the community not as facts which make them worth shunning, but as grounds for giving them special care and attention. With such care and attention, there is hope for individuals in remedial forms of education and therapy which will give them a share in the basic human goods. Thus they will be able to partake of some measure of human flourishing. In some respects these seem modest hopes, though judged against the ways in which these folk have been treated in the past, they will take much effort on the part of the disabled and their supporters to realise. The religious alternative promises a great deal more, but it embodies a thought that some might see as dangerously delusive: namely that by some magic wave of the divine wand *this person* who is autistic or Down's or whatever can be transformed and their disability washed away.

Ethics and inarticulacy

It has been part of the aim of this study to show that the ethical problems surrounding the cognitively disabled cannot be isolated from the deepest issues which touch all of our lives, whether we have any contact with the disabled or not. One reason why this is so is brought out by Charles Taylor's idea of a 'moral framework'.[25] A moral framework consists in a set of strong moral evaluations and qualitative distinctions which give shape to our moral thought and to our actions. These will be evaluations and distinctions relating to what we think makes for a full life, for respect and dignity, and what we consider our most important moral obligations to consist in. The pure and mixed utilitarian philosophers whom we have argued with in previous chapters are revealed to have a moral framework in which the capacity for certain rich kinds of experience is the source of strong moral evaluations. The importance of the cognitively disabled for moral philosophy is that they force moralists to become articulate about their frameworks, that is make explicit the character of the strong evaluations which mould their thinking. Taylor's point is that moral thinking and action at any time is only possible given that some strong evaluations and distinctions or other are then in place.

There is a strong moral evaluation which I have argued is revealed by an acceptable ethics for the cognitively disabled. It is that spelled out in Simone Weil's assertion of the moral equality of all human beings. This evaluation is integrally connected to a qualitative distinction in our acts and practices. It is the distinction between prizing or praising people for their merits, achievements or specific qualities and prizing them as human beings. Both forms of prizing relate to granting dignity and respect to others and both are connected to the demands of justice. But prizing someone as a human being is the source of a unique kind of respect and dignity insofar as it is invariant between human beings because it is grounded in the possession of mere humanity.

So we have the idea of the cognitively disabled as forcing us to be articulate about our moral frameworks. Taylor's treatment of these themes raises the further question of how articulate must a viable morality be about the moral framework it presupposes. The religious, theistic thinker wants us to be articulate about the strong moral evaluations inherent in Simone Weil's claims for human dignity. We should be articulate to the extent that we locate, via metaphysics, that property of the human which is the ground of seeing a fundamental good in all human beings, a good which does not depend on merits, achievements or specific qualities. Taylor himself airs the idea that our reaction to murder depends on some 'ontology of the human' or other.[26] He toys with the charge that the only ontology of the human which will do the trick is the theistic one, specifically the Christian affirmation that all are worthy of loving respect because all are creatures of a God who gives that respect to all.[27] He asks these questions of secular alternatives:

> Is the naturalist affirmation [of the dignity of human beings] conditional on a vision of human nature in the fullness of its health and strength? Does it move us to extend help to the irremediably broken, such as the mentally handicapped, those dying without dignity, foetuses with genetic defects? Perhaps one might judge that that it doesn't and that this is a point in favour of naturalism. But the careers of Mother Teresa or Jean Vanier point to a different pattern, emerging from Christian spirituality.[28]

Having, so to speak, refreshed the theological challenge by reference to Taylor, we can now recap on the answer provided to it. We should note first that we do not have to appeal to a tradition of Christian, or any other, spirituality to ground unselfish care for the disabled. We can see the sense of the worth of any and every human being in the care and love provided by Vicky's mum and dad. We can see it in the dedication of the teacher in the special school or in the work of the speech therapist with an autistic child. These modes of care make manifest the claim of the afflicted human being upon those open to that claim. Our sense of the authenticity of the response of these human beings is the ground of the affirmation made by Weil. To point to these responses and those things to which they are connected in human life (such as the fact that human beings have names and that any human being is someone's child) is to suggest a way of being articulate about the strong evaluation implicit in the Weil affirmation. It is not, however, a metaphysical articulacy. Taylor is right to point to some forms of naturalism making the dignity of the human being dependent on his/her being 'in the fullness of health and strength'. We have to ask, however, whether the falseness of that way of approaching the matter is more firmly shown by pointing to 'traditions of spirituality' and the metaphysical claims they rest on or by bringing to mind the many and varied ways in which we recognise the other as a human being. This question gains force from two points brought out in this chapter. The metaphysics of theism ground the relation of human creature to God in participation in a moral drama and telos from which many human beings are precisely excluded by their disability. In addition, the love God has for all his creatures, human and non-human, is quite obviously compatible with God so arranging creation that very many of these creatures live and die afflicted.

We have not by any means exhausted the religious dimensions to the ethics of the cognitively disabled. Let us consider again Cora Diamond's point that in some peasant communities the disabled are regarded as touched by God and as God's gift to their families.[29] There is a sense in which we can say that the cognitively disabled are uniquely valuable in the sight of God, even though we do not endorse a theistic metaphysics in so doing. This sense is outlined for us in Stewart Sutherland's conception of theological language as marking out for us a perspective on things *sub specie aeternitatis*.[30] Integral to Sutherland's conception is that theological language can function in a regulative fashion in human life. Rather than describe an object for us, it can make possible and encourage lines of reflection and questioning in relation to human affairs. One particular line of reflection it encourages centres on the need to see a worth and value in objects and actions which is independent of my individual needs and interests, or of the interests and needs of the group I happen to belong to. So talk of trying to see and value things as they are in God's eyes is a continual spur to rise above individual and local interests in valuing things. Now this is precisely what we are called upon to do in relation to the cognitively disabled. If I judge them by the contribution they make to the furthering of my interests or the interests of my community, I am liable to think that they lack merit and worth. Indeed, they will be seen as having a negative value, contributing little in positive terms to my own or my group's material interests while being a charge upon me and others. They will tend to lack what the particular interests of my society regard as achievements and as success-making properties. So I must stand back from these individual and local interests to see their worth. This worth rests chiefly on their status as my fellow human beings. They invite me, therefore, to accept that the foundation of worth does not depend on something contingent to a person: what s/he happens to contribute to what happen to be the interests of my group. Rather it depends on something essential to a human being – nothing other than his/her humanity. This source of worth makes us all equal in foundational worth. In God's eyes, we are all equal. From the standpoint of eternity, there is no difference amongst us. The cognitively disabled are a gift from God insofar as they are a revelation of the fact which is the source of our eternal worth: the fact that nothing but mere humanity is the source of that worth. Whenever I feel the tendency to regard worth as a function of what contributes to my individual advancement or my group's interests, the disabled are a continual reminder that this tendency represents merely a local, limited standpoint which needs to be transcended in the final analysis.

How far are we to take the idea of forming an idea of the worth of things and people from a standpoint *sub specie aeternitatis*? It is clear that both secular moral philosophers and theologians want to transcend not merely the view of things from the standpoint of my individual interests or of the interests of my local group. They want a perspective on value 'from the centre of the universe', as I have described it. This entails a necessary grounding of moral perceptions in facts and principles somehow more central and certain than our shared human nature and our fundamental moral reactions as human beings. This is a perspective which I have argued is not available to us. Its unavailability is bound up, on the one hand, with the fact that reason, moral reason in particular, is immanent in its employment and grounds and, on the other, with the nature of humanism as a perspective. But there is something in these efforts to transcend a human perspective which must be respected. Sutherland's idea is that the standpoint *sub specie aeternitatis* is a necessary regulative idea. So we should always be open to reasoned objections to the way we think and act morally. In particular, it is not a requirement of recognising the immanence of reason and the importance of humanism that we endorse the ways human beings have adopted of behaving toward non-human animals and to the environment generally. It remains my contention that all such matters are left open by the arguments of this book.

Notes

Preface

1. Simone Weil *The Need for Roots*, pp. 15–16. I am indebted to Jean Curthoys' *Feminist Amnesia*, p. 13 for this reference.

1 The Philosophical Problem

1. See Stephen Clark's writings for an example, particularly *The Moral Status of Animals*.
2. See J. Smith and K. Boyd eds *Lives in the Balance* for an appropriate case.
3. Glover *Causing Death and Saving Lives*, p. 50.
4. Sumner *Abortion and Moral Theory*, pp. 37–8.
5. Sumner *Abortion and Moral Theory*, p. 38.
6. For a properly detailed case for the conclusion that rationality is underpinned by intelligence see Bennett's *Rationality*, pp. 80–94.
7. 'Autonomy and the value of human life', p. 54.
8. 'Autonomy and the value of life', p. 54. The same argument is given in Frey's 'Animal parts and animal wholes' and 'The significance of agency and marginal cases'.
9. This is the argument of such books as Rawls' *A Theory of Justice* and Gauthier's *Morals by Agreement*. A summary of the case can be found in Byrne *The Philosophical and Theological Foundations of Ethics*, pp. 80 ff.
10. *Morals by Agreement*, p. 268.
11. *A Theory of Justice*, p. 505.
12. As Rawls does in *A Theory of Justice*, p. 509.
13. For a summary of difficulties in contractarianism see Byrne *The Philosophical and Theological Foundations of Ethics*, pp. 92 ff.
14. *Causing Death and Saving Lives*, p. 82.
15. Utilitarianism has developed responses to this kind of objection to its application. The question at issue is whether they work. For a survey see Byrne *The Philosophical and Theological Foundations of Ethics*, pp. 76 ff.
16. *The End of Life*, pp. 24–5.
17. *The End of Life*, pp. 57–8.
18. *The End of Life*, p. 77.
19. *The End of Life*, pp. 64–5.
20. 'Animal parts and animal wholes', p. 97. A similar case for vivisection on human beings is also to be found in Singer's 'Unsanctifying life', pp. 47–8.
21. 'Animal parts and animal wholes', p. 96.
22. 'Animal parts and animal wholes', p. 97.
23. *Causing Death and Saving Lives*, p. 163. The conclusion rests on the point that to kill a baby is not to violate autonomy – *Causing Death and Saving Lives*, pp. 156–8.

24. I paraphrase *Causing Death and Saving Lives*, p. 122.
25. *Causing Death and Saving Lives*, pp. 163–4.
26. *Causing Death and Saving Lives*, p. 164.
27. *Should the Baby Live?*, pp. 164–70.
28. See *Should the Baby Live?*, p. 115.
29. Most famously in Duff and Campbell's 'Moral and ethical dilemmas in the special care nursery'. For further references see *Should the Baby Live?* and the papers in Horan and Delahoyde *Infanticide and the Handicapped New Born*.
30. See Boddington and Podpadec 'Who are the mentally handicapped?' for a detailed exploration of this point.
31. *The End of Life*, p. 59.
32. Just such an argument for the necessity of religious ethics is found in Mitchell's *Morality: Religious and Secular*, Ch. 9.

2 Defining Mental Handicap

1. *International Classification of Impairments, Disabilities and Handicaps*, quoted in Lindzey *Dictionary of Mental Handicap*, p. 92.
2. *Dictionary of Mental Handicap*, p. 169.
3. *A Gentle Touch*, pp. 31–2.
4. As noted by Kavale and Forness *The Science of Learning Difficulties*, pp. 45–6.
5. Pat Henton 'Caring', in Brechin and Walmsley *Making Connections*, p. 159.
6. Ashton and Ward *Mental Handicap and the Law*, p. 12. The criterion that cognitive disability is permanent, while mental illness is temporary, is crude. It relates to a more precise point to emerge later in the section: cognitive disability is a defect *of* or *in* development (while mental illness, if manifested early in life, may merely *affect* development).
7. See for example the data in Richardson and Koller 'Epidemiology', in Clarke, Clarke and Berg *Mental Deficiency*, pp. 371–2.
8. *Mental Handicap and the Law*, pp. 15–16 and 18–19.
9. 'Mental retardation in non-western societies', in Haywood *Socio-Cultural Aspects of Mental Retardation*, and *Mental Retardation*, pp. 116–18.
10. 'Mental retardation in non-western societies', p. 534.
11. 'Mental retardation in non-western societies', p. 538.
12. 'Mental retardation in non-western societies', p. 532.
13. *A Gentle Touch*, p. 34.
14. *A Gentle Touch*, pp. 32–3.
15. The arguments which follow are heavily indebted to Boorse 'On the distinction between illness and disease', in Cohen, Nagel and Scanlon *Medicine and Moral Philosophy*.
16. See *Dictionary of Mental Handicap*, p. 38 for examples.
17. Evans and Waites *IQ and Mental Testing*, pp. 120–3.
18. *Classification in Mental Retardation*, p. 11.
19. *Classification in Mental Retardation*, p. 11.
20. Hence there is a debate around the scientific suitability of social adaptiveness serving as a criterion for cognitive disability. For a summary and critique of the case against the AAMD's diagnostic scheme see Clarke and

Clarke 'Criteria and classification', in Clarke, Clarke and Berg *Mental Deficiency*, pp. 47–8.

21. *Classification in Mental Retardation*, p. 24.
22. Hagberg and Hagberg 'Commentary', in Dobbing *Scientific Studies in Mental Retardation*, p. 14.
23. See, for example, Berger and Yule 'IQ tests and assessment', in Clarke, Clarke and Berg *Mental Deficiency*, Evans and Waites *IQ and Mental Testing* and K. Richardson *Understanding Intelligence*.
24. Frith *Autism*, p. 90.
25. Berger and Yule 'IQ tests and assessment', p. 66.
26. Beveridge 'Commentary', in Dobbing *Scientific Studies in Mental Retardation*, p. 365.
27. See Evans and Waites *IQ and Mental Testing* and Mercer *Labelling the Retarded* for the elements of this case at greater length.
28. *Labelling the Retarded*, pp. 2 ff.
29. See K. Richardson *Understanding Intelligence* for support for this point.
30. For these data see: Jordan and Powell *Understanding and Teaching Children with Autism*, pp. 156–7, Schreibman *Autism*, p. 25 and Wing 'Diagnosis, clinical description', in Wing *Early Childhood Autism*, p. 40.
31. See Boucher 'What could possibly explain autism?', in Carruthers and Smith *Theories of Mind*, p. 224.
32. Harris 'Pretending and planning', in Baron-Cohen, Flusberg and Cohen *Understanding Other Minds*, p. 240.
33. See Frith *Autism* for an account of these pioneering experiments, pp. 159–61.
34. Data and summary are due to Perner 'The theory of mind deficit in autism', in Baron-Cohen, Flusberg and Cohen *Understanding Other Minds*, p. 119.
35. Klin and Volkmar 'The development of individuals with autism', in Baron-Cohen, Flusberg and Cohen *Understanding Other Minds*, pp. 324–5.
36. See the papers by: Mundy, Sigman and Kasari; Tager-Flausberg; Hobson; and Gómez, Sarriá and Tamarit, in Baron-Cohen, Flusberg and Cohen *Understanding Other Minds*.
37. Volkmar and Klin 'Social development in autism', in Baron-Cohen, Flusberg and Cohen *Understanding Other Minds*, pp. 44–5.
38. See Boucher 'What could possibly explain autism?', pp. 225–6.
39. See Wing 'Epidemiology and theories of aetiology', pp. 70 ff.
40. Frith *Autism*, pp. 76–7.
41. See Leslie and Roth 'What autism teaches us about metarepresentation', in Baron-Cohen, Flusberg and Cohen *Understanding Other Minds*, for an example of this kind of theorising.
42. As in Gordon and Barker 'Autism and the theory of mind debate', in Graham and Stephens *Philosophical Psychopathology*.
43. *Autism*, pp. 92–104. It is notable that the testimony of able autistics supports the notion that the autistic experience the world (not just the social world) as a chaotic and disordered set of stimuli and find it difficult to detach their attention from individual stimuli and see their place in the whole. See the moving autobiographical testimonies of Donna Williams and Alison Hale in the Bibliography.
44. See *Autism and the Development of Mind*.
45. *Dictionary of Mental Handicap*, p. 210.

46. Corbett 'Psychiatry and mental retardation', in Dobbing *Scientific Studies in Mental Retardation*, p. 484.
47. Hagberg and Hagberg 'Prevention of pre-, peri- and postnatal brain pathology', in Dobbing *Scientific Studies in Mental Retardation*, p. 54.
48. The papers in Zigler and Balla *Mental Retardation* explore the issues surrounding this hypothesis.
49. Richardson 'Commentary', in Dobbing *Scientific Studies in Mental Retardation*, pp. 18–23.
50. Nine per cent of males with an IQ between 35 and 60: *Dictionary of Mental Handicap*, p. 125.
51. 'Epidemiology', in Clarke, Clarke and Berg *Mental Deficiency*, pp. 357–8.
52. Fombone 'Prevalence of autistic spectrum disorder in the UK', p. 229.
53. Smeets and Lascioni 'Acquisition of non-vocal communication', p. 375. Higher estimates for the linguistic competence of the autistic are found (as in Jordan and Powell *Understanding and Teaching Children with Autism* p. 52). It is possible that varying results of research on this point reflect the different ways in which the autistic population may be defined and sampled.

3 The Moral Status of the Cognitively Disabled

1. *Causing Death and Saving Lives*, p. 58.
2. *The End of Life*, p. 148.
3. *The End of Life*, p. 150.
4. See Gaita *Good and Evil*, pp. 13–14.
5. This point is demonstrated fully by Maclean in *The Elimination of Morality*, pp. 24–6.
6. 'The importance of being human', pp. 56–7.
7. *A Theory of Justice*, p. 505.
8. *A Theory of Justice*, p. 506.
9. See Kuhse and Singer *Should the Baby Live?*, pp. 121–3. The same move will be found in Glover *Causing Death and Saving Lives*, p. 50 and Singer 'Can we avoid assigning greater value to some human lives than others?', pp. 93–4.
10. See Williams *Ethics and the Limits of Philosophy*, pp. 118–19. Hence, whatever 'animal liberation' is it is not like black or women's liberation, since animals cannot be liberated from the psychic oppression caused by negative attitudes towards them. Many of the cognitively disabled, in contrast to animals, can feel the negative attitudes towards them and suffer from the way those attitudes encourage lack of self-respect. See Williams and Shoultz *We Can Speak for Ourselves*. More on the nature of oppression in Chapter 5.
11. *Ethics and the Limits of Philosophy*, p. 118.
12. For an example of this case see Clark 'Animal wrongs', p. 149.
13. These facts are set out fully in Kagan's *The Second Year*.
14. *Should the Baby Live?*, p. 133.
15. 'The definition of "person"', p. 175.
16. I derive this argument from Teichman 'The definition of "person"'.
17. As argued by Ruse in *Taking Darwin Seriously*, pp. 103 ff. and Flew *Darwinian Evolution*, pp. 46–9.
18. Flew defends the idea of a common human nature from within an evolutionary perspective in *Darwinian Evolution*, pp. 67 ff.

19. It is common to rest this case on the possibility of teaching captive chimpanzees and gorillas sign language. The precise significance of these experiments should, however, be weighed carefully. See the discussions of ape-language and communication skills in Leahy *Putting Animals into Perspective* and Dupré 'Conversations with apes', in Hyman *Investigating Psychology*.
20. Clark 'Environmental ethics', in Byrne and Houlden *Companion Encyclopedia of Theology*, pp. 55–6. Clark resists the line of reasoning he summarises, but only because he postulates Cartesian, immaterial minds to supervene on the material things we call human beings.
21. *Autism*, pp. 17 ff.
22. See *The Value of Life*, pp. 14 ff.
23. See *The Elimination of Morality*, pp. 26–9.
24. Cf. *The Elimination of Morality*, p. 5.
25. A point made forcibly in Gaita *Good and Evil*, pp. 26–9.
26. Diamond 'Eating meat and eating people', p. 469.
27. The theme of relationship rather than monadic properties being the ground of respect for others is explored by many contemporary writers. Mutual love as the ground of respect for the disabled is affirmed by Pailin, *A Gentle Touch*, pp. 106–7. What follows in this chapter and in Chapter 6 will be seen to be both similar and dissimilar to Pailin's approach.
28. Hence the moral absurdity in the claims of a Glover that the reason why killing babies is generally wrong is the prevention of outrage to the feelings of parents and relatives, *Causing Death and Saving Lives*, pp. 163–4: as if those attitudes were not called forth by their object. This is to liken the killing of a baby to the killing of a pet.
29. See Devine *The Ethics of Homicide*, pp. 15–17.
30. For an extended defence of the account of moral concepts I am drawing upon see Brennan *The Open Texture of Moral Concepts*. The implications of this account of moral concepts for our understanding of 'human being' which follow are derived from the discussion of the concept in Cockburn's *Other Human Beings*.
31. See for example Dent *Rousseau* (*passim*) and Rawls *A Theory of Justice*, p. 440.
32. Cf. *A Theory of Justice*, pp. 463–5.
33. Hauerwas *Suffering Presence*, p. 169.

4 Euthanasia, Abortion and Genocide

1. At greatest length in Kuhse and Singer *Should the Baby Live?* See also Rachels *The End of Life* and Glover *Causing Death and Saving Lives*.
2. The description which follows is drawn from *Should the Baby Live?*, pp. 1–11, Kennedy 'R. v. *Arthur, Re B* and the severely disabled new-born child', pp. 154–5, and Linacre Centre *Euthanasia and Clinical Practice*, pp. 85–8.
3. See 'R. v. *Arthur, Re B* and the severely disabled new-born child', pp. 155–60.
4. See 'R. v. *Arthur, Re B* and the severely disabled new-born child', pp. 157–8.
5. *The New Genocide of Handicapped and Afflicted People*, p. 69.
6. See Weir *Selective Nontreatment of Handicapped New-Borns*, pp. 131 ff.
7. Lamb *Down the Slippery Slope*, p. 11.

8. For passionate advocacy of the analogy see Wolfensberger's *The New Genocide of Handicapped and Afflicted People* and the essays in Horan and Delahoyde *Infanticide and the Handicapped New-Born*. For an account of the defence against the charge and a judicious summing up see Lamb *Down the Slippery Slope*, Ch. 2.
9. For evidence on the eugenics movement see Clarke 'Criteria and classification', in Clarke, Clarke and Berg *Mental Deficiency*, pp. 30–1 and Evans and Waites *IQ and Mental Testing*, pp. 8–11.
10. *Disability: Whose Handicap?*, p. 89.
11. *Should the Baby Live?*, pp. 97–117.
12. *Should the Baby Live?*, p. 138.
13. *Should the Baby Live?*, p. 117.
14. A claim which forms the burden of Wolfensberger's case in *The New Genocide of Handicapped and Afflicted People*.
15. See Lamb *Down the Slippery Slope*, p. 120.
16. *The Ethics of Homicide*, p. 16.
17. *The End of Life*, p. 77.
18. A contrary view on the relation between murder and justice will be found in *The Ethics of Homicide*, pp. 31–2, but Devine appears to have a narrower notion of justice in mind.
19. *Should the Baby Live?*, p. 170.
20. Cf. *Down the Slippery Slope*, pp. 99–100.
21. *Should the Baby Live?*, pp. 169–70.
22. As Hagberg and Hagberg in 'Aspects of prevention', in Dobbing *Scientific Studies in Mental Retardation* explain, p. 54.
23. Gibson *Down's Syndrome*, p. 281.
24. See 'Animal parts, human wholes', p. 92 and 'The significance of agency', p. 40.
25. *The Elimination of Morality*, pp. 122–5.
26. Quoted in Kennedy 'R. v. *Arthur, Re B* and the severely disabled new-born child', p. 160.
27. As argued by Maclean *The Elimination of Morality*, pp. 129–30.
28. *Selective Nontreatment of Handicapped New-Borns*, pp. 205–15.
29. *Selective Nontreatment of Handicapped New-Borns*, p. 207.
30. *The Ethics of Homicide*, pp. 24–30.
31. Gibson *Down's Syndrome*, p. 32.
32. As Weir's survey of paediatric policies amply bears out: *Selective Nontreatment of Handicapped New-Borns*, pp. 61–87.
33. 'R. v. *Arthur, Re B* and the severely disabled new-born child', p. 161.
34. 'R. v. *Arthur, Re B* and the severely disabled new-born child', p. 161.
35. Henton 'Caring', in Brechin and Walmsley *Making Connections*, p. 159.
36. See, for example, *The New Genocide of Handicapped and Afflicted People*, pp. 68–9.
37. See Gibson *Down's Syndrome*, p. 282.
38. Jakobovitz *Jewish Medical Ethics*, p. 183.
39. Jakobovitz 'The status of the embryo', in Dunstan and Seller *The Status of the Human Embryo*, p. 65.
40. 'The status of the embryo', p. 66.
41. 'The status of the embryo', p. 67.

42. See Byrne 'The animation tradition', in Dunstan and Seller *The Status of the Human Embryo*, pp. 98–9 for an outline of this argument.
43. See Becker 'Human being' in Cohen, Nagel and Scanlon *Medicine and Moral Philosophy*, pp. 32–4.
44. For the arguments behind these assertions see Miller *A Most Unlikely God*, pp. 31–3 and the references there cited.

5 Cognitive Disability and Oppression

1. Sinason *Mental Handicap*, p. 2.
2. In Ryan *The Politics of Mental Handicap*, Chs 2, 3 and 4. Frank Thomas's testimony shows that many of those classed as cognitively disabled feel the negative evaluation of them expressed in such harsh treatment. Hence, one of the most important movements in recent years has been the attempt by the cognitively disabled to fight the way in which they are perceived, to make their own voice heard and thereby to demand the respect that is due to them. See Williams and Schultz *We Can Speak for Ourselves* for an account of the self-advocacy movement.
3. Quoted in Kurtz 'The sociological approach to mental retardation', in Brechin, Liddiard and Swain *Handicap in a Social World*, p. 16 and Clarke and Clarke 'Criteria and classification', in Clarke, Clarke and Berg *Mental Deficiency*, pp. 30–1.
4. The account which follows is indebted to the discussion of oppression in Curthoys *Feminist Amnesia*, pp. 18–29 and 32–6, and hers in turn to Franzt Fanon *The Wretched of the Earth* and Paulo Freire *The Pedagogy of the Oppressed*.
5. As Gooding in *Disabling Laws, Enabling Acts* claims, p. 13.
6. Edgerton 'Mental retardation in non-western societies', in Haywood *Socio-Cultural Aspects of Mental Retardation*, p. 526.
7. Diamond 'Rights, justice and the retarded', in Kopleman and Moskop *Ethics and Mental Retardation*, pp. 57–9.
8. Edgerton 'Mental retardation in non-western societies', pp. 533–4.
9. 'What's in a name?', in Brechin and Walmsley *Making Connections*, p. 76.
10. 'What's in a name?', p. 79.
11. A fact amply demonstrated in Evans and Thwaites *IQ and Mental Testing*.
12. 'What's in a name?', pp. 79–80.
13. *Disabling Laws, Enabling Acts*, p. 11.
14. *Labelling the Mentally Retarded*, p. 28. For a summary and references to social labelling theory as applied to the cognitively disabled see Gove 'The labelling perspective: an overview' and Gordon 'Examining labelling theory: the case of mental retardation', in Gove *The Labelling of Deviance* and the papers by Emerson and McGill and Emerson in Brown and Smith *Normalisation*.
15. See Roth and Kroll *The Reality of Mental Illness*, especially pp. 15–17 and Gove 'Labelling and mental illness: a critique' in Gove *The Labelling of Deviance*.
16. For a very brief overview of the critical literature see McGill and Emerson 'Normalisation and applied behaviour analysis' in Brown and Smith *Normalisation*, pp. 64–5 and the papers in Gove *The Labelling of*

Deviance, especially Gordon 'Examining labelling theory: the case of mental retardation'.

17. 'Historical and legal aspects', in Kirman and Bicknell *Mental Handicap*, pp. 8–9.
18. See, for example, pp. 73–5 for a debunking of talk of the special needs of children.
19. *A Sociology of Special Education*, pp. 104–5.
20. For a summary and critique of these Foucauldian ideas about knowledge see Freadman and Miller *Re-Thinking Theory*, pp. 166 ff.
21. See for example *A Sociology of Special Education*, p. 26.
22. See *A Sociology of Special Education*, pp. 174–5.
23. *Disabling Laws, Enabling Acts*, p. 12.
24. *Stigma*, p. 12.
25. Saflios-Rothschild 'Disabled persons' self-definitions', in Brechin, Liddiard and Swain *Handicap in a Social World*, p. 6.
26. Bogdan and Taylor 'What's in a name?', p. 79.
27. *Disability: Whose Handicap?*, p. 10.
28. See *Disability: Whose Handicap?*, pp. 138–50.
29. For this case see the previous reference to Shearer and Meazzini 'Mainstreaming handicapped students', in Dobbing *Scientific Studies in Mental Retardation*. It is also linked to Tomlinson's critique of special education cited above.
30. For a much fuller summary of Wolfensberger's normalisation philosophy see Emerson 'What is normalisation?', in Brown and Smith *Normalisation*.
31. Szives 'The limits to integration', in Brown and Smith *Normalisation*.
32. See Robinson 'Normalisation: the whole answer?', in Brechin and Walmsley *Making Connections*.
33. Yule 'Commentary', in Dobbing *Scientific Studies in Mental Retardation*, p. 545.
34. Szives provides evidence for the occurrence of this possible effect of mainstreaming, 'The limits to integration?', pp. 119–21.
35. For evidence against this particular application of labelling theory see Clarke and Clarke 'Criteria and classification', p. 42.
36. See Mittler 'Evaluation of services and staff training', in Dobbing *Scientific Studies in Mental Retardation*, pp. 554–6.
37. See the papers in *Normalisation* for accounts of the Scandinavian school and Perrin and Nirje 'Setting the record straight', in Brechin and Walmsley *Making Connections* for a firsthand account of this version of the normalisation philosophy.
38. See Rose-Ackerman 'Mental retardation and society', p. 81.
39. See *The Foundations of Justice*, pp. 3 ff.
40. My account will draw upon Brown *Modern Political Philosophy*, Ch. 6, Finnis *Natural Law and Natural Rights* and Galston *Justice and the Human Good*.
41. As argued by Galston *Justice and the Human Good*, pp. 121–31.
42. See Finnis *Natural Law and Natural Rights*, pp. 186–8.
43. See *The Foundations of Justice*, Ch. 5 for the essence of this argument.
44. See *Anarchy, State and Utopia*, pp. 32–3.
45. *A Theory of Justice*, pp. 311–12.
46. It may be possible to so modify Rawls' theory as to bring non-rational,

non-self-conscious agents into the terms of the contract. See Vandeveer 'Of beasts, persons and the original position'.
47. Galston *Justice and the Human Good*, p. 5.
48. Compare Brown *Modern Political Philosophy*, p. 159 with Finnis *Natural Law and Natural Rights*, pp. 86–9 and with Galston *Justice and the Human Good*, pp. 58 ff.
49. Brown *Modern Political Philosophy*, p. 159.

6 Theological and Religious Issues

1. *Morality: Religious and Secular*, p. 123.
2. *Morality: Religious and Secular*, p. 129.
3. *Morality: Religious and Secular*, pp. 126–8.
4. *Morality: Religious and Secular*, p. 128.
5. *Morality: Religious and Secular*, p. 134.
6. *Morality: Religious and Secular*, p. 134.
7. Compare Gaita *Good and Evil*, p. 128.
8. *A Gentle Touch*, p. 63.
9. *A Gentle Touch*, p. 116.
10. *A Gentle Touch*, p. 118.
11. *A Gentle Touch*, p. 119.
12. 'Human being, individual and social', in Gunton *The Cambridge Companion to Christian Doctrine*, p. 159.
13. *Death and Eternal Life*, pp. 49–50.
14. 'Human being, individual and social', p. 166.
15. The brief account which follows is taken from Leget's summary of Aquinas' views in *Living with God*.
16. 'Human being, individual and social', p. 166.
17. 'Human being, individual and social', p. 176.
18. 'Human being, individual and social', p. 177.
19. See Fergusson 'Eschatology', in Gunton *The Cambridge Companion to Christian Doctrine*, pp. 230–1 and 237–8.
20. *Death and Eternal Life*, pp. 158–61 and 165–6.
21. *A Gentle Touch*, pp. 159–60.
22. See Churchill 'Philosophical and theological perspectives on the value of the retarded', in Kopleman and Moskop *Ethics and the Mentally Retarded*, p. 179.
23. Pailin appears to argue otherwise: *A Gentle Touch*, pp. 43–4.
24. *Death and Eternal Life*, p. 160.
25. See *Sources of the Self*, pp. 25 ff., for what follows.
26. *Sources of the Self*, p. 5.
27. *Sources of the Self*, pp. 515–16.
28. *Sources of the Self*, p. 517. Jean Vanier founded the L'Arche communities for the cognitively disabled.
29. 'Rights, justice and the retarded', in Kopleman and Moskop *Ethics and the Mentally Retarded*, pp. 57–9.
30. In his *God, Jesus and Belief*. I draw particularly on pp. 83–6.

Bibliography

G. Ashton (with A. Ward) *Mental Handicap and the Law* (London: Sweet and Maxwell, 1992)

L. C. Becker 'Human being' in M. Cohen, T. Nagel and T. Scanlon eds *Medicine and Moral Philosophy* (Princeton: Princeton University Press, 1981) 23–48

J. Bennett *Rationality* (London: Routledge, 1964)

M. Berger and W. Yule 'IQ tests and assessment' in A. M. Clarke, A. D. B. Clarke ᵃnd J. M. Berg eds *Mental Deficiency*, Fourth Edition (London: Methuen, 1985) 53–96

M. C. Beveridge 'Commentary' in J. Dobbing ed. *Scientific Studies in Mental Retardation* (London: Macmillan and Royal Society of Medicine, 1984) 365–6

P. Boddington and T. Podpadec 'Who are the mentally handicapped?', *Journal of Applied Philosophy*, vol. 8 (1991) 177–99

R. Bogdan and S. J. Taylor 'What's in a name?' in A. Brechin and J. Walmsley eds *Making Connections* (London: Hodder and Stoughton, 1989) 76–81

C. Boorse 'On the distinction between illness and disease' in M. Cohen, T. Nagel and T. Scanlon eds *Medicine and Moral Philosophy* (Princeton: Princeton University Press, 1981) 3–23

J. Boucher 'What could possibly explain autism?' in P. Carruthers and P. Smith eds *Theories of Theories of Mind* (Cambridge: Cambridge University Press, 1996) 223–41

J. M. Brennan *The Open Texture of Moral Concepts* (London: Macmillan, 1977)

A. Brown *Modern Political Philosophy* (Harmondsworth: Penguin, 1986)

P. Byrne 'The animation tradition' in G. R. Dunstan and M. J. Seller eds *The Status of the Human Embryo* (London: King's Fund Press, 1988) 86–110

——*The Philosophical and Theological Foundations of Ethics* (London and Basingstoke: Macmillan, 1992)

L. R. Churchill 'Philosophical and theological perspectives on the value of the retarded' in L. Kopelman and J. C. Moskop eds *Ethics and Mental Retardation* (Dordrecht: Reidel, 1984) 177–82

S. R. L. Clark 'Animal wrongs', *Analysis*, vol. 38 (1978) 147–9

——'Environmental ethics' in P. Byrne and J. L. Houlden eds *A Companion Encyclopedia to Theology* (London: Routledge, 1995) 843–68

——*The Moral Status of Animals* (Oxford: Clarendon Press, 1984)

A. M. Clarke and A. D. B. Clarke 'Criteria and classification' in A. M. Clarke, A. D. B. Clarke and J. M. Berg eds *Mental Deficiency*, Fourth Edition (London: Methuen, 1985) 28–30

D. Cockburn *Other Human Beings* (London and Basingstoke: Macmillan, 1990)

J. A. Corbett 'Psychiatry and mental retardation' in J. Dobbing ed. *Scientific Studies in Mental Retardation* (London: Macmillan and Royal Society of Medicine, 1984) 479–90

J. Curthoys *Feminist Amnesia* (London: Routledge, 1997)

N. J. H. Dent *Rousseau* (Oxford: Blackwell, 1988)

P. E. Devine *The Ethics of Homicide* (Ithaca: Cornell University Press, 1978)

C. Diamond 'Eating meat and eating people', *Philosophy*, vol. 53 (1978) 465–79
—— 'The importance of being human' in D. Cockburn ed. *Human Beings* (Cambridge: Cambridge University Press, 1991) 37–62
—— 'Rights, justice and the retarded' in L. Kopelman and J. C. Moskop eds *Ethics and Mental Retardation* (Dordrecht: Reidel, 1984) 7–62
R. S. Duff and A. G. M. Campbell 'Moral and ethical dilemmas in the special care nursery', *New England Journal of Medicine*, vol. 289 (1973) 890–4
J. Dupré 'Conversations with apes' in J. Hyman ed. *Investigating Psychology* (London: Routledge, 1991) 95–116
R. Edgerton *Mental Retardation* (Glasgow: Fontana, 1979)
—— 'Mental retardation in non-western societies' in H. C. Haywood ed. *Socio-Cultural Aspects of Mental Retardation* (New York: Appleton-Century-Crofts, 1970) 523–59
E. Emerson 'What is normalisation?' in H. Brown and H. Smith eds *Normalisation: a Reader for the Nineties* (London: Routledge, 1992) 1–18
B. Evans and B. Waites *IQ and Mental Testing* (London and Basingstoke: Macmillan, 1981)
F. Fanon *The Wretched of the Earth* (Harmondsworth: Penguin, 1967)
D. Fergusson 'Eschatology' in C. E. Gunton ed. *The Cambridge Companion to Christian Doctrine* (Cambridge: Cambridge University Press, 1997) 226–44
J. Finnis *Natural Law and Natural Rights* (Oxford: Clarendon Press, 1980)
A. Flew *Darwinian Evolution*, Second Edition (London and New Brunswick, NJ: Transaction Publishers, 1997)
E. Fombone 'Prevalence of autistic spectrum disorder in the UK', *Autism*, vol. 1 (1997) 227–9
R. Freadman and S. Miller *Re-Thinking Theory* (Cambridge: Cambridge University Press, 1994)
P. Freire *The Pedagogy of the Oppressed* (Harmondsworth: Penguin 1996)
R. Frey 'Animal parts and animal wholes' in J. M. Humber and R. F. Almeder eds *Biomedical Ethics Reviews* (Clifton, NJ: The Humana Press, 1987) 89–107
—— 'Autonomy and the value of life', *The Monist*, vol. 70 (1987) 50–63
—— 'The significance of agency and marginal cases', *Philosophica* vol. 39 (1987) 39–46
U. Frith *Autism* (Oxford: Blackwell, 1989)
R. Gaita *Good and Evil* (London and Basingstoke: Macmillan, 1980)
W. A. Galston *Justice and the Human Good* (Chicago: University of Chicago Press, 1980)
D. Gauthier *Morals by Agreement* (Oxford: Clarendon Press, 1986)
D. Gibson *Down's Syndrome* (Cambridge: Cambridge University Press, 1978)
J. Glover *Causing Death and Saving Lives* (Harmondsworth: Penguin 1977)
E. Goffman *Stigma* (Harmondsworth: Penguin, 1968)
J. C. Gómez, E. Sarriá and J. Tamait 'The comparative study of early communication and theories of mind' in S. Baron-Cohen, H. Tager-Flusberg and D. J. Cohen eds *Understanding Other Minds* (Oxford: Oxford University Press, 1993) 397–426
C. Gooding *Disabling Laws, Enabling Acts* (London: Pluto Press, 1994)
R. A. Gordon 'Examining labelling theory: the case of mental retardation' in W. R. Gove ed. *The Labelling of Deviance* (Beverly Hills and London: Sage, 1980) 111–225

R. M. Gordon and J. A. Barker 'Autism and the theory of mind debate' in G. Graham and G. L. Stephens eds *Philosophical Psychopathology* (Cambridge, MA: MIT Press) 163–81

W. R. Gove 'Labelling and mental illness' in W. R. Gove ed. *The Labelling of Deviance* (Beverly Hills and London: Sage, 1980) 58–109

—— 'The labelling perspective: an overview' in W. R. Gove ed. *The Labelling of Deviance* (Beverly Hills and London: Sage, 1980) 9–33

H. J. Grossman ed. *Classification in Mental Retardation* (Washington, DC: American Association on Mental Deficiency, 1983)

B. Hagberg and G. Hagberg 'Commentary' in J. Dobbing ed. *Scientific Studies in Mental Retardation* (London: Macmillan and Royal Society of Medicine, 1984) 13–17

—— 'Aspects of prevention of pre-, peri- and post-natal brain pathology in severe and mild mental retardation' in J. Dobbing ed. *Scientific Studies in Mental Retardation* (London: Macmillan and Royal Society of Medicine, 1984) 43–56

A. Hale *My World Is Not Your World* (Ingateston, Essex: Archimedes Press, 1998)

P. Harris 'Pretending and planning' in S. Baron-Cohen, H. Tager-Flusberg and D. J. Cohen eds *Understanding Other Minds* (Oxford: Oxford University Press, 1993) 228–46

S. Hauerwas *Suffering Presence* (Edinburgh: T. and T. Clark, 1988)

P. Henton 'Caring' in A. Brechin and J. Walmsley eds *Making Connections* (London: Hodder and Stoughton, 1989)

J. Hick *Death and Eternal Life* (London: Collins, 1976)

P. Hobson *Autism and the Development of Mind* (Hove and Hillsdale: Lawrence Erblaum, 1993)

—— 'Understanding persons' in S. Baron-Cohen, H. Tager-Flusberg and D. J. Cohen eds *Understanding Other Minds* (Oxford: Oxford University Press, 1993) 204–27

D. J. Horan and M. Delahoyde eds *Infanticide and the Handicapped New-Born* (Provo: Brigham Young University Press, 1982)

I. Jakobovitz *Jewish Medical Ethics* (New York: Bloch, 1975)

—— 'The status of the embryo in the Jewish tradition' in G. R. Dunstan and M. J. Seller eds *The Status of the Human Embryo* (London: King's Fund Press, 1988) 62–73

R. Jordan and S. Powell *Understanding and Teaching Children with Autism* (Chichester: John Wiley and Sons, 1995)

J. Kagan *The Second Year* (Cambridge, MA: Harvard University Press, 1981)

K. A. Kavale and S. R. Forness *The Science of Learning Difficulties* (Windsor: NFER-Nelson, 1985)

I. M. Kennedy 'R. v. Arthur, Re B, and the severely disabled new-born baby' in I. M. Kennedy, *Treat Me Right* (Oxford: Clarendon Press, 1988) 154–74

B. Kirman 'Historical and legal aspects' in B. Kirman and J. Bicknell eds *Mental Handicap* (Edinburgh: Churchill Livingstone, 1975) 3–30

A. Klin and F. Volkmar 'The development of individuals with autism' in S. Baron-Cohen, H. Tager-Flusberg and D. J. Cohen eds *Understanding Other Minds* (Oxford: Oxford University Press, 1993) 317–31

H. Kuhse and P. Singer *Should the Baby Live?* (Oxford: Oxford University Press, 1985)

R. A. Kurtz 'The sociological approach to mental retardation' in A. Brechin, P. Liddiard and J. Swain eds *Handicap in a Social World* (Sevenoaks: Hodder and Stoughton, 1981) 16–23

D. Lamb *Down the Slippery Slope* (London: Croom Helm, 1988)

M. P. T. Leahy *Putting Animals into Perspective* (London: Routledge, 1991)

C. Leget *Living with God* (Leuven: Peeters, 1997)

A. Leslie and A. Roth 'What autism teaches us about metarepresentation' in S. Baron-Cohen, H. Tager-Flusberg and D. J. Cohen eds *Understanding Other Minds* (Oxford: Oxford University Press, 1993) 82–111

Linacre Centre *Euthanasia and Clinical Practice* (London: Linacre Centre, 1982)

M. P. Lindsey *Dictionary of Mental Handicap* (London: Routledge, 1989)

A. Maclean *The Elimination of Morality* (London: Routledge, 1993)

P. McGill and E. Emerson 'Normalisation and applied behaviour analysis' in H. Brown and H. Smith eds *Normalisation: a Reader for the Nineties* (London: Routledge, 1992) 60–83

P. Meazzini 'Mainstreaming handicapped students' in J. Dobbing ed. *Scientific Studies in Mental Retardation* (London: Macmillan and Royal Society of Medicine, 1984) 527–40

J. Mercer *Labelling the Retarded* (Berkeley: University of California Press, 1974)

B. Miller *A Most Unlikely God* (Notre Dame: University of Notre Dame Press, 1996)

B. G. Mitchell *Morality: Religious and Secular* (Oxford: Clarendon Press, 1980)

P. Mittler 'Evaluation of services and staff training' in J. Dobbing ed. *Scientific Studies in Mental Retardation* (London: Macmillan and Royal Society of Medicine, 1984) 547–67

P. Mundy, M. Sigman and C. Kasari 'The theory of mind and joint attention deficits in autism' in S. Baron-Cohen, H. Tager-Flusberg and D. J. Cohen eds *Understanding Other Minds* (Oxford: Oxford University Press, 1993) 181–203

R. Nozick *Anarchy, State and Utopia* (Oxford: Blackwell, 1974)

D. Pailin *A Gentle Touch* (London: SPCK, 1992)

J. Perner 'The theory of mind deficit in autism' in S. Baron-Cohen, H. Tager-Flusberg and D. J. Cohen eds *Understanding Other Minds* (Oxford: Oxford University Press, 1993) 112–37

B. Perrin and B. Nirje 'Setting the record straight' in A. Brechin and J. Walmsley eds *Making Connections* (London: Hodder and Stoughton, 1989) 220–8

J. Rachels *The End of Life* (Oxford: Oxford University Press, 1986)

J. Rawls *A Theory of Justice* (Oxford: Oxford University Press, 1972)

K. Richardson *Understanding Intelligence* (Milton Keynes: Open University Press, 1990)

S. A. Richardson 'Commentary' in J. Dobbing ed. *Scientific Studies in Mental Retardation* (London: Macmillan and Royal Society of Medicine, 1984) 17–23

S. A. Richardson and H. Koller 'Epidemiology' in A. M. Clarke, A. D. B. Clarke and J. M. Berg eds *Mental Deficiency*, Fourth Edition (London: Methuen, 1985) 356–400

T. Robinson 'Normalisation: the whole answer?' in A. Brechin and J. Walmsley eds *Making Connections* (London: Hodder and Stoughton, 1989) 247–52

S. Rose-Ackerman 'Mental retardation and society', *Ethics*, vol. 92 (1982) 81–101

M. Roth and J. Kroll *The Reality of Mental Illness* (Cambridge: Cambridge University Press, 1986)

M. Ruse *Taking Darwin Seriously* (Oxford: Blackwell, 1986)

J. Ryan *The Politics of Mental Handicap* (Harmondsworth: Penguin, 1980)

C. Saflios-Rothschild 'Disabled persons' self-definitions and their implications for rehabilitation' in A. Brechin, P. Liddiard and J. Swain eds *Handicap in a Social World* (Sevenoaks: Hodder and Stoughton, 1981) 5–13

L. Schreibman *Autism* (Newbury Park, CA: Sage, 1988)

A. Shearer *Disability: Whose Handicap?* (Oxford: Blackwell, 1981)

V. Sinason *Mental Handicap and the Human Condition* (London: Free Association Books, 1992)

P. Singer 'Can we avoid assigning greater value to some human lives than others?' in R. S. Laura and A. F. Ashman eds *Moral Issues in Mental Retardation* (London: Croom Helm, 1985) 93–4

—— 'Unsanctifying life' in J. Ladd ed. *Ethical Issues Relating to Life and Death* (Oxford: Oxford University Press, 1979) 41–61

P. M. Smeets and G. E. Lascioni 'Acquisition of non-vocal communication and discrimination learning' in J. Dobbing ed. *Scientific Studies in Mental Retardation* (London: Macmillan and Royal Society of Medicine, 1984) 375–92

J. Smith and K. Boyd eds *Lives in the Balance* (Oxford: Oxford University Press, 1991)

L. W. Sumner *Abortion and Moral Theory* (Princeton: Princeton University Press, 1981)

S. R. Sutherland *God, Jesus and Belief* (Oxford: Blackwell, 1984)

S. Szives 'The limits to integration' in H. Brown and H. Smith eds *Normalisation: a Reader for the Nineties* (London: Routledge, 1992) 112–31

H. Tager-Flusberg 'What language reveals about the understanding of minds in children with autism' in S. Baron-Cohen, H. Tager-Flusberg and D. J. Cohen eds *Understanding Other Minds* (Oxford: Oxford University Press, 1993) 138–57

C. Taylor *Sources of the Self* (Cambridge: Cambridge University Press, 1989)

J. Teichman 'The definition of "person"', *Philosophy*, vol. 60 (1985) 175–85

S. Tomlinson *A Sociology of Special Education* (London: Routledge, 1982)

M. Tooley *Abortion and Infanticide* (Oxford: Clarendon Press, 1983)

D. Vandeveer 'Of beasts, persons and the original position', *The Monist*, vol. 62 (1979) 368–77

K. Vanhoozer 'Human being, individual and social' in C. E. Gunton ed. *The Cambridge Companion to Christian Doctrine* (Cambridge: University Press, 1997) 158–88

H. Veatch *The Foundations of Justice* (New York: Oxford University Press, 1986)

F. R. Volkmar and A. Klin 'Social development in autism' in S. Baron-Cohen, H. Tager-Flusberg and D. J. Cohen eds *Understanding Other Minds* (Oxford: Oxford University Press, 1993) 40–55

S. Weil *The Need for Roots* (London: Routledge, 1978)

R. F. Weir *Selective Nontreatment of Handicapped New-Borns* (New York: Oxford University Press, 1984)

B. Williams *Ethics and the Limits of Philosophy* (London: Fontana, 1985)

D. Williams *Nobody, Nowhere* (New York: Avon Books, 1992)

—— *Somebody, Somewhere* (London: Transworld Books, 1995)

P. Williams and B. Schultz *We Can Speak for Ourselves* (London: Souvenir Press, 1982)

L. Wing 'Diagnosis, clinical description, and prognosis' in L. Wing ed. *Early Childhood Autism* (Oxford: Pergamon Press, 1976)

——'Epidemiology and theories of aetiology' in L. Wing ed. *Early Childhood Autism* (Oxford: Pergamon Press, 1976) 65–92

W. Wolfensberger *The New Genocide of Handicapped and Afflicted People* (Syracuse, NY: Author, 1987)

W. Yule 'Commentary' in J. Dobbing ed. *Scientific Studies in Mental Retardation* (London: Macmillan and Royal Society of Medicine, 1984) 544–6

E. Zigler and D. Balla eds *Mental Retardation* (Hillsdale, NJ: Lawrence Erlbaum, 1982)

Index

M